of related interest

Asperger's Syndrome
A Guide for Parents and Professionals
Tony Attwood
Foreword by Lorna Wing
ISBN 1 85302 577 1

The Little Class with the Big Personality
Experiences of Teaching a Class of Young Children with Autism
Fran Hunnisett
ISBN 1 84310 308 7

Specialist Support Approaches to Autism Spectrum
Disorder Students in Mainstream Settings
Sally Hewitt
ISBN 1 84310 290 0

Asperger Syndrome – What Teachers Need to Know
Matt Winter
Written for Cloud 9 Children's Foundation
ISBN 1 84310 143 2

Incorporating Social Goals in the Classroom
A Guide for Teachers and Parents of Children with
High-Functioning Autism and Asperger Syndrome
Rebecca A. Moyes
Foreword by Susan J. Moreno
ISBN 1 85302 967 X

Addressing the Challenging Behaviour of Children with
High-Functioning Autism/Asperger Syndrome in the Classroom
A Guide for Teachers and Parents
Rebecca A. Moyes
ISBN 1 84310 719 8

Teaching Children with Autism and Related Spectrum Disorders
An Art and a Science

Christy L. Magnusen

Foreword by Tony Attwood

Jessica Kingsley Publishers
London and Philadelphia

First published in 2005
by Jessica Kingsley Publishers
116 Pentonville Road
London N1 9JB, UK
and
400 Market Street, Suite 400
Philadelphia, PA 19106, USA

www.jkp.com

Library of Congress Cataloging in Publication Data
Magnusen, Christy
    Teaching children with autism and related spectrum disorders : an art and a science /
Christy L. Magnusen ; foreword by Tony Attwood
        p. cm
    Includes bibliographical references.
    ISBN-13: 978-1-84310-747-7 (pbk. : alk. paper)
    ISBN-10: 1-84310-747-3 (pbk. : alk. paper) 1. Autistic children--Education. 2. Autism.
I. Title.
    LC4717.M32 2005
    371.94--dc22
                                                    2005009444

British Library Cataloguing in Publication Data
A CIP catalogue record for this book is available from the British Library

ISBN-13: 978 1 84310 747 7
ISBN-10: 1 84310 747 3

Printed and Bound in Great Britain by
Athenaeum Press, Gateshead, Tyne and Wear

This book could not have reached print without the assistance of many individuals: family, friends, colleagues and parents. Each has served to guide, inspire, and cheer me on. I am very grateful.

However, as simple as it may seem, this book has reached completion, in large part, because of the influence of one little boy. Now a grown man, Johnny was one of the first students with autism that I encountered when I began my career. In typical fashion of children with autism, he was often heard to use echolalia. There are many theories and ideas about why individuals repeat what they hear, and although there are probably many reasons that drive this behavior, I have come to know that while their words may not be their own, their message may be communicative, even symbolic. Johnny opened that door for me during my first year of teaching, when he would sing the opening lines of the (then popular) song "People" (Styne and Merrill 1968), once recorded by Barbra Streisand. Johnny's fascination with a song that centered around people and their relationships always struck me with irony. As I would soon realize, helping him to learn to relate and need other people would be one of the most difficult challenges I faced.

Johnny's repetition of these lyrics, and their inherent message was prophetic. They became central to my own understanding about how to reach children with autism, and galvanized my efforts to help others teach them. It is my belief that the largest and most pervasive characteristic of autism lies in the social realm, and the successes (or lack of progress) in developing and maintaining relationships is our greatest obstacle. Social gracefulness is the key to success at home, at work, at school, and in any of the other communities to which we belong. Because autism throws up so many barriers in how a child with autism develops, functions, and is perceived, it is paramount that those who are responsible for their care keep the focus encouraging their ability to socialize.

This book is therefore dedicated to Johnny, who by his innocent rendition of the words of a song, showed me the way. Thank you, J.W., this book is for you!

Christy

Acknowledgment

My heartfelt thanks must be acknowledged in print to my dear colleague and friend, Ms Ann Delaney. She willingly took on the enormous challenge of transferring my written words onto a typed manuscript in preparation for the publication of this book.

Thank you, Ann, for your patience, perseverance, efficiency, and extraordinary attention to detail.

Contents

List of boxes, tables, and figures

Boxes

Tables

Figures

Foreword

Christy Magnusen has worked with many children with varying degrees of autism over several decades and has been in hundreds of classrooms. She has read, analysed and applied in the classroom the main theoretical texts for education, speech therapy and autism. She has theoretical knowledge and practical experience as well as a level of enthusiasm, dedication and creativity that make her an exceptional therapist and specialist in autism. Christy also has an intuitive insight into how an autistic child thinks, communicates and learns. If I had a child with autism, I would want Christy Magnusen to be my child's teacher or therapist.

Her intention in writing this book was to help people be hopeful and excited about teaching children with autism. She has certainly succeeded. The explanations of theoretical models and practical strategies will improve the abilities and confidence of teachers and thereby improve the quality of life of children with autism and their parents. Christy rightly considers that teaching children with autism is an art and a science, a mixture of theatre and theory. As I read her book I became infected with her enthusiasm and inspired by her recommendations. She really understands autism and what to do in the classroom.

This book is essential reading for teachers and parents, and will be their guide to the range of educational options suitable for a particular child, taking into account that child's profile of abilities and learning style. Although this may be a small volume, I know that the practical experience, wisdom and talent of the author, which is so evident throughout, will ensure that this book will be referred to many times and become one of the key texts on teaching children with autism.

Tony Attwood

Preface

Children with autism are more a part of our society than ever before. The features of what we now call the autism spectrum are better understood and therefore recognized earlier and confused less with other conditions. While autism has always cut across racial, social, economic, and geographic boundaries, we now see autism in some form repeat itself more than once in many families. Yet the complexity of the autistic spectrum disorders (ASDs) continues to challenge us. While many race for a cure, the immediate caretakers, parents, physicians, teachers, therapists, friends, and family must find a way to deal with, reach, and teach them. Despite the fact that we are more skilled than ever at detecting autism, we are still searching for viable ways to teach children who have it. Educators and families often find themselves at odds over this issue. Children with autism are as diverse as they are similar, and this is perplexing to the most experienced teacher. Their unique learning rates and learning styles demand highly prescriptive and individualized approaches. Many teachers are unprepared for working with children on the autism spectrum. They may either lack pre-service training, or have had limited experience with autism.

The process of creating an effective, appropriate educational program is difficult at best, never easy, and often an arduous one. As one parent remarked to me at an IEP (Individual Education Plan) meeting, "We're in a marathon, aren't we?" His metaphor is an insightful one.

This book was written to assist anyone and everyone who desires to teach children with autism. Even though its content and intended audience are fairly specific, this book would not have come about if it were not reflective in some way of the broader contexts of philosophy, social science, linguistics, and psychology. I salute the many great masters whose discoveries, theories, observations, and wisdom have shaped our ideas about how children learn, think, and communicate.

Autism can be perplexing and frustrating, because it is relentless. Children who have autism may seem to be moving targets because although the condition is pervasive, it changes developmentally. It is still difficult to determine (with precision) if these children change because of their autism or because of our intervention.

For all of these reasons, teachers may find this a formidable assignment. This book was designed to help teachers and parents appreciate that success in teaching is a combination of science and artistry. Having knowledge about techniques and strategies is only one half of the task. Teachers must have a keen sense of timing, of creativity, and intuition. Teaching is both an art and a science. It is far more than what you take away from an in-service, or the degree that you earned in college. Children with autism require us to use this approach, perhaps as much or more than other children.

This book was written to help people be hopeful and excited about teaching children with autism. The approaches outlined in the following pages rest upon the presumption that all humans are connected in a fundamental way and because of this innate connection they are reachable. Their unique learning styles require us to adjust our teaching styles:

> The natural world evokes our awe by the specialized designs of its creatures and their parts. We don't poke fun at the eagle for his clumsiness on the ground or fret that the eye is not very good at hearing, because we know that a design can excel at one challenge only by compromising at others. (Pinker 1997, p.565)

CHAPTER 1

The Big Picture

Professionals are dealing with a fragile entity, parental hope.
(Hart 1995, pp.58–59)

Bringing up and educating children is indeed a humbling experience. There has never been a shortage of theories on how to do so. Who would dispute the reputations of Dr. Spock, John Dewey, or Horace Mann? Yet, practical, everyday experience with children is an illuminating one: one which does not always follow the textbooks.

Parents and teachers of all children have an important moral and ethical responsibility; and it is best when we face this responsibility together. We create the lens through which our children see the world. We shape their thinking process, their social patterns, and their knowledge base. We organize and prioritize their growing minds. Finally, we germinate their opinions and their values. We bolster their self-esteem, and modify prejudices. Through our overt enthusiasm (or our covert silence), we get them ready for the world.

When we determine what children should learn, we must do so with conscientious deliberation and forethought. The outcome of their education is directly related to this process. This is an overwhelming task for everyone, but it is an especially daunting one when mapping the education for children with special needs.

Children learn what parents, teachers, and schools want them to. Most school communities are now able to gauge with precision and predictability the scope, sequence, and learning rate of the majority of its learners. This is a phenomenal, if not unimaginable, accomplishment. Unfortunately, students with autism are not very predictable. In fact, they are consistently inconsistent, and this makes teaching them a challenge.

For centuries, civilized societies have attempted to bring peace and harmony among people with diverse views, opinions, and actions. However, those individuals outside a given set of norms are essentially viewed as different – they look different, act different, talk different. An outgrowth of this phenomenon is to have conformity, to change those who are outside the norm to fit within the norm. The term "different" often carries the connotation of "wrongness," "unacceptable," and "exclusion."

People with autism have never fit within most norms. In his book, *Extraordinary People* (2000), Darold Treffert cautions us: "In dealing with handicapped persons, whatever the handicap, we need to accommodate to their needs and specialness rather than requiring them to make all the changes – to become exactly like us – if they expect to live side by side with us in our communities" (p.327).

People on the autism spectrum are not without gifts and talents. Their autism is so striking that we may see their differences before we can appreciate their capabilities. People with autism now have the right to live, learn, and work among others. But to do so requires special understanding, help, and support. To accomplish this, we are required to stretch those boundaries of "normal," of what is acceptable, allowed, and appreciated.

CHAPTER 2

How Children with Autism Think and Learn

> Any sensible theory of autism must be compatible with what we know about brain development. (Frith 2003, p.205)

The degree to which our learning (and our behavior) can be shaped or altered by events in the environment has fueled a long-standing debate over how and why humans are the way they are. The literature is consumed with ideas and theories about how people learn and think (Bandura 1969; Caine and Caine 1997; Dewey 1998; Gardner 1987b, 1991; Greenspan and Wieder 1998; Montessori 1967; Pinker 1997; Skinner 1974; Sylwester 1995; Vygotsky 1962). Essentially, the final, complete answer to how the "typical" mind develops and functions continues to elude us. We are even farther from understanding how children with autism see the world, why they react the way they do, and how much we can change them through the teaching process. Contemporary neuroscientists are sifting through the complex and dynamic interchange between the psycho-social, biological, and environmental factors which influence human behavior. Creationists are not convinced that we are who we are without a divine presence. Yet we know that humans are not static beings. They change and adapt, somehow, to their world. This book does not pretend to reveal the precise formula for how much of our learning capacity is fixed, or how much it can be changed through environmental influence, but it does make sense to acknowledge the involvement of both extremes, for it seems it could never be one to the exclusion of the other. Our biological endowment certainly sets the stage for our capacity to learn, and for who we might become. Our immediate surroundings undoubtedly shape our individual templates. This is important to those of us who face a child with autism every day, whether at home or at school. If we were to accept the position that our biological-genetic inheritance rendered us immune to external influence, children with autism would most certainly be doomed, for they would never be capable of overcoming their challenges.

Although we are almost certain that the neurobiological mechanism in children with autism is atypical, we do not know why or how their minds work the way they do. Why is socialization so difficult? What accounts for the wide variability in their intellectual capacities? Why do some develop speech, and others remain mute?

It appears that there may be multiple abnormalities in the way they receive, process, organize, store, retrieve, and use information. These difficulties seem to occur in different degrees and combinations in children across the spectrum, and for these reasons, autism rarely affects children in exactly the same way. However, because of the way their brains function, children with autism will always appear qualitatively different in almost any context. Understanding this basic difference is vital to teachers because from this realization they must adjust, in large part, how they teach. Although we cannot change the fact that a child has autism, we can be hopeful that he or she will respond to what we set before him or her in the classroom.

The attention given recently to the notion of "brain-based" learning and instruction makes sense for students with autism. Brain-based learning theorists recognize that not all children are neurologically the same. In fact some (probably those with autism) are hardwired quite differently (Armstrong 1987, 1998; Caine and Caine 1997; Gardner 1987a; Lazear 1991; Sylwester 1995). Brain-based learning theory supports the concept that although children's brains may be biologically hardwired, they are still responsive and pliable to environmental stimuli. Caine and Caine's (1997) position is that children's brains are not segmented into separate units which are responsive to discrete domains such as math, or science, or language. Rather, children learn wholistically, and there is cross-over in information processing that occurs throughout the brain known as patterning, Caine and Caine believe that the learning and teaching process must be individually matched for each student. Their twelve learning principles provide us with a conceptual model for recognizing the way a child's brain operates and how it can ultimately influence how he learns. Some of these fundamental principles, according to Caine and Caine (1997), suggest that the brain is an adaptive system and that learning is developmental and ongoing. This is a hopeful idea for teachers who face children with autism, as it suggests that their condition is not static, but changeable. In other words, they are teachable. Caine and Caine also maintain that each brain is organized in a unique manner, and that we process, acquire, and remember information in different ways as well. Patterning is a concept that is fundamental to brain-based learning theorists because it suggests that we are able to reach (at least some children) through repetition of information. Children with autism, many of whom cling to sensory experiences, are often susceptible to learning new information when their sensory experiences have a routine element to them. Most of us know either through trial and error or astute planning, that the more we "pattern" or structure our students with autism, the more routine and predictable we make their environments, and the more they seem to learn. Finally, advocates of the brain based learning model recognize that our brain is a "social brain." In neuro-typically organized children, we can see this every day in many ways, as we observe children who can take what they have learned and place it correctly within a social context. For our students with autism, this is a much more arduous task, but it provides us with an over-arching explanation for the difficulties they face at school.

CHAPTER 3

Putting Theory into Practice

> Before I got married I had six theories about bringing up
> children; now I have six children and no theories. (John Wilmot,
> Earl of Rochester, "Letters," quoted in Macaulay 1994, p.186)

Once it is accepted that a child has autism, it is vitally important to
set in motion supports that will assist him or her. Autism is pervasive.
It affects a person, continuously, throughout his or her life span: at
home, school, and in the community. In concert with parents, schools
are often the first to be called upon to assist a child. More often than
not, a child with autism will need special help in order to learn,
especially to master social situations and communicate in meaningful
ways. In her recent discussion of the essential components of an
educational program for children with autism, Uta Frith (2003,
pp.218–219) lists the following:

1. The treatments that work have the belief that this is a
   condition that will not go away.

2. Improvements can be expected over the course of a lifetime.

3. There is an underlying neurological condition that is
   untreatable.

4. Explicit learning will occur despite the fact that implicit
   learning may fail.

5. A behavioral approach as a listener and as a speaker is
   important when dealing with one who has autism.

6. Caregivers must be ingenious.

7. Learning occurs by association.

8. Caregivers should understand the condition of autism.

I would certainly support Frith's guidelines. Anyone new to program development or teaching children with autism would do well to ascribe to them. However, as with any theoretical belief or general principles, translating them meaningfully into daily practice is hard because they are, by their nature, broad. How they translate into daily context may seem overwhelming to a school faculty new to autism.

All educators face the proverbial quandary of putting theory into practice. Sometimes it is possible; at other times it is maddening. I hope that the theme of this book will provide schools and families with suggestions for instructions that are well thought out and feasible from both a theoretical as well as a practical point of view.

Historical perspectives

Early in my career, because of my background and interest in language development, I was convinced that teaching children with autism to talk was the key to success (theirs and mine!). In fact many of the first published learning programs had this emphasis as well (Hewett 1965; Kozloff 1973; Lovaas 1969, 1977). So certain was I that these theorists and I were correct, I forged ahead and developed a noteworthy collection of nouns, verbs, and adjectives in my students' vocabularies and I measured our progress in numbers: "Johnny now has 15 action verbs, one present participle, four prepositions, three opposites, and 45 nouns." One day I was approached by a parent (not Johnny's), and she took me aside: "Christy, you are such a good speech therapist…but my son doesn't use any of the words you taught him!" I was dumbfounded. That evening I pored over my data sheets, examining percentages and notes that I thought demonstrated this student's mastery level. It took me a while, but I eventually realized what this well-intended, very wise lady was trying to tell me: my theory did not match what I should do (for her child) in practice.

What I know now is that there are about four general goals, which if emphasized properly during the school years have an especially positive impact on a student with autism:

- to reach a state of independence
- to develop spontaneous communication in social situations
- to be capable of self-advocacy and decision making
- to apply academic knowledge in a functional way.

In the end, it is really not the number of words a child learns but how and when he or she uses them that will make a difference. Once I realized this, I immediately shifted priorities and learned to focus on (what we now call) developing pragmatic language, or the child's ability to communicate in practical useful ways. I also realized that it was their lack of understanding of social rules and expectations that was their overarching problem, not their language proficiency. In *Thinking in Pictures* (1995), Temple Grandin reinforces this concept: "Throughout my life, I have always been helped by understanding teachers and mentors. People with autism desperately need guides to instruct and educate them so they will survive the social jungle" (p.19).

Fortunately, we are much more advanced about the methods and best practices used to teach children with autism than when I started out. Unfortunately, however, these advancements have been accompanied by methodological debates, resulting in educational litigation between schools and parents who are in dispute over which instructional strategies are appropriate. The National Research Council's recent text, *Educating Children with Autism* (2001) responded to this issue and reviewed ten of the most well-known programs in the United States. These programs generally fell within one or two categories in their theoretical approach: development and behavior (some had features of both). The following were considered essential:

- early and intensive treatment
- family involvement
- highly trained staff
- ongoing assessment
- systematic instruction
- highly supportive staffing environments
- emphasis on communication
- plans for generalization and maintenance
- individualized programs.

These key points make sense, and they are general enough to allow flexibility in the choice of instructional methodology. Yet we know getting a program up to speed to meet these standards is a formidable task.

The art and science model: A new best practice

In my years of experience, I have come to realize that it is the teachers, therapists, and other interventionists who make the biggest difference in the autistic child's ability to learn. Methods, theories, strategies, and instructional practices are important, but it is the teachers' creative use of these techniques, not the teachers themselves, that make a difference. As Temple Grandin notes: "I am indebted to good teachers…who ran old-fashioned classrooms with lots of opportunities for interesting hands-on activities…my teachers [also] encouraged my creativity…as I grew older, the people who were of the greatest assistance were always the more creative, unconventional types" (1995, pp.95–99).

In a perfect world, all teachers would have the ability, the energy, the resources, the enthusiasm, and the creativity to teach all children, including those with autism. In reality, this is rarely the case. Very few teachers have had pre-service training to learn the theories and strategies they will need to use with a child on the autism spectrum. Likewise, most have had no (or limited) first-hand experience of actually teaching them, and so they must learn through trial and error. This is frustrating to everyone – parents, teachers, and children – because it slows down or impedes the process. We came to realize that teachers needed special training to help them reach a child with autism. Yet my observations and experiences in training and program development revealed that they needed more than a list of techniques and strategies in order to be successful.

I had spent the greatest part of my career mentoring and coaching teachers, and upon reflection, realized that many of our in-services and training sessions failed. The teachers did not fail, the trainers did. I am a firm believer that, with rare exceptions, teachers truly want to help children succeed, yet I was confounded by the fact that some were far more effective than others. I thought long and hard about this and came to the conclusion that those individuals who ultimately master this job are those who can combine theory with practice in a creative, intuitive way. Their sense of timing, control, and approach with children is always astonishing to me. Many of them may be "book smart," but all of them are artists. Simply put: the atmosphere, tempo, and organization of their classroom is a haven for a child with autism. And I know it when I see it.

The idea for this book seeped into my consciousness years ago. So many teachers were seeking information about their new autistic students. The demand for training, workshops, and in-service flooded the country. If I could just bottle the talent that I had seen in those master teachers and give it to others, it would be a wonderful thing. It was then that I became aware that merely listing all the techniques and methods they could use would be meaningless because it would be incomplete. I realized then that these master teachers had another quality, and a very important one. It was a talent that I certainly did not give them or teach them, but I recognized it and cultivated it, nevertheless.

The idea of the "art and science" model of teaching children emerged from this realization. If I can help teachers and other staff understand this concept, they will almost surely be successful. They will learn to use their scientific knowledge about autism and learning theory in the right way, with the right child, at the right time.

CHAPTER 4

An Integrated Approach

A theory of education could only be derived from under-standing the mind that is to be educated. (Premack and Premack 2003, p.227)

Autism cannot be explained easily and we should know that. But I see people mistakenly do this all the time. I have frequently heard the remark: "He's testing you" (a behaviorist), or "She is doing that because she can't communicate" (a language therapist), or "He should know better, he has an IQ over 120, and he told the clerk that she was overweight, middle-aged, and stupid" (Asperger comment to a clerk who probably is middle-aged and overweight). Simply put, autism is much more complex than most realize.

When I am called upon to help teachers understand autism, from the beginning I tell them that working with autism is like manipu-lating a Rubik's cube – there are three main dimensions, with many facets to each dimension. The behavior of a child with autism is not easily explained through one dimension, nor can it be dealt with with a quick intervention. As with a Rubik's cube, autism should be regarded as three dimensional, each of the dimensions affecting the other two.

Autism is also not a static condition. It is a moving target and it changes developmentally over time and with intervention. When a feature of autism changes, the rest of its features change accordingly. In my opinion, it is best viewed as a dynamic combination and interchange of communication, adaptive behavior, and sensory integration issues. Sometimes, one, two or all three influence how a child with autism appears. Understanding and accepting this will give teachers a better grasp of how to approach their students. If one confines her view of autism to, perhaps, a behaviorist explanation, for why her student does what he does, she may miss the fact that his behavior is a result of his trying to communicate with her. Likewise, he may be reacting in this way because of a sensory integration default. Programs which focus exclusively on only one of these three features short-change the child in the long run, because in reality he is a composite of all three. He can learn to cope with them with our help.

I believe a student is best served when a program acknowledges this and keeps these three features in dynamic balance. We frequently see that if we adjust behavioral expectations or alter the nature of a sensory experience, we see positive changes in attention, focus, and language usage. Likewise, when a child develops the ability to communicate, there is a corresponding improvement in previously unexplainable behavioral outbursts. A change in one dimension serves as a catalyst in another.

In the following sections, you will find three of the major theoretical orientations used in designing an appropriate program for a student with autism: behaviorism, social communication, sensory integration. The most effective program combines all three.

Behaviorism

O. Ivar Lovaas has long been associated with a behavioristic approach for teaching children with autism. Actually the "Lovaas method" is a reflection of the earlier studies completed by Pavlov, Watson, and Skinner. Although Lovaas may be the most prominent, there are numerous theorists and clinicians who support the behaviorist model (Hamblin *et al.* 1971; Harris and Weiss 1998; Hewett 1965; Koegel and Koegel 1996; Kozloff 1973; LaVigna and Donnellan 1986;

Maurice 1993; Maurice, Green, and Luce 1995). Programs th
behavioral principles have much in common, but may use va
terms to describe their methods. Discrete trial training, behavior
modification, behavior management, and applied behavior analysis
are actually quite similar because they include most if not all of the
following strategies:

- Overt behavior can be altered, changed, or modified by
  manipulating certain environmental conditions.

- Learning is actually an outcome of this methodological theory.

- This approach is divided into three clear components:
  Stimulus, Response, Consequence (or reinforcement) – S–R–C.

- This technique is teacher driven, and highly prescriptive: the
  teacher begins and ends this three-part exchange (stimulus and
  consequence), the child responds.

- This method rests on the idea that children can learn through
  association – they make a connection between the stimulus,
  response, and consequence.

- Behavior that is reinforced will occur again.

- The more a behavior is reinforced, the stronger it will become.

- A behavior that is not reinforced will cease to exist.

- Over-use of reinforcement will diminish its effectiveness.

I have seen the popularity of behaviorism wax, wane, and wax again.
I believe there is a place for these methods in the overall scope of a
program model. I also believe there are certain children with certain
learning objectives that are better served by other techniques. What I
have experienced is that behaviorism is not for every child, nor
should it be used forever or in isolation. I have categorized behaviorist methods into those I regard as being most and least effective.
These guidelines should be viewed as flexible definitions and not
mutually exclusive of one another. A behavioral approach is most
beneficial when used with:

- young children just entering school
- children who are considered lower functioning
- children who are overly active and/or who have problems remaining focused
- when a concept or skill is initially introduced (novelty level)
- when a concept or skill is very complex or difficult.

A behavioral approach is less effective when:

- teaching social-pragmatic language
- instructing higher functioning students
- the goal is maintenance or generalization of a skill
- the goal is independent or spontaneous demonstration of a skill.

It is important to understand that some behavioral techniques are best used under certain conditions. They demand considerable time, energy, and creativity. Teachers/therapists whose instructional style incorporates these techniques are clearly using a behaviorist approach. Box 4.1 lists 15 of the primary techniques with corresponding prescription for best practice.

Behavioral strategies for children with autism have numerous merits, the most important being that they immediately impose a structured template for the learning environment. Target behaviors are usually meticulously defined; questions, directives, and consequences are prepared in advance. Data collection boosts the accountability of these programs. The child's responses are consistently recorded and analyzed against antecedent events, the stimulus and the consequences. Progress is charted in a step-by-step manner. Errors are analyzed so the program can be adjusted.

Some teachers use behavioral strategies naturally. They are truly the artists at changing behavior. Other teachers have to "practice" using these techniques, and that's okay. What everyone needs to remember is that when we modify children's behavior we help them

Box 4.1 Behaviorism techniques

Technique	*Best practice*
1. Alternative changes in behavior typically take two or three weeks (10 to 15 school days) and only when the chosen intervention is used consistently.	1. This is a long stretch for most people. You must be patient and consistent.
2. Using continuous reinforcement (or consequence) will bring about a change in behavior more quickly.	2(a). Apply the consequence each and every single time the behavior occurs. 2(b). Timing of reinforcement used on a continuous schedule should be immediate – within three to five seconds of the child's response.
3. Choose highly motivating reinforcers.	3(a). Think out-of-the-box in learning what the child likes. 3(b). Reinforcers can be edible and tangible (primary) or social (secondary) in nature. 3(c). Ask parents and school bus drivers for ideas.
4. Attention (verbal, physical, visual) is a powerful motivator.	4. Attention is your cheapest reinforcement. Use it wisely. How you look, stand, talk can either reinforce or deter a behavior.
5. Reinforcement can be positive or it can be negative.	5(a). Positive reinforcement should be used to increase the strength or probability of occurrence of a desired target behavior. 5(b). Negative reinforcement (such as ignoring) can be used to deter a behavior – it is the withdrawal of reinforcement until a desire behavior occurs.
6. Use fading reinforcement once a behavior is established. This will maintain it over time.	6. Be careful not to drop reinforcement too drastically. Rather, use a gradual approach (reinforce nine out of ten, then seven out of ten, then four out of ten responses).

7. High frequency behaviors are best managed by an immediate and continuous intervention.

7. High frequency behaviors are "expressive" to the classroom. A reduction of 50 percent may not seem like much, but it is dramatic and substantial to bring this about.

8. Ignore a behavior that is sudden, unexpected, or extreme in nature.

8. Never ignore a behavior that is dangerous or a life-safety issue.

9. Avoid using contingencies that leave you with no alternative (e.g., "If you don't finish your math, you can't go home").

9. Use "if – then" only if "it doesn't matter" (e.g., "If you take a bite of that chicken, you can have a bite of that marshmallow").

10. Catch them being good! Behavioral programs should focus (equally) on appropriate behavior as well as inappropriate behavior.

10. This has the same effect as intermittent reinforcement. It will maintain a behavior.

11. Use clear, concise, firm directions.

11. Avoid "psychoanalysis." Get to the point without using extra words or rationales.

12. Antecedent events (those that occur before or at the same time as the stimulus) could be important.

12. We know that there are other "triggers" that impact behavior, besides the S–R–C technique. Antecedent events often reveal those sensory integration or communication factors.

13. Build "alternative" behaviors to replace the ones that are inappropriate.

13. Avoid saying "no," "don't," or "stop." Rather say "Put your hands down."

14. Define target behaviors in an objective manner.

14. Use observable, measurable words to allow you to "see" and "count" behaviors.

15. List and prioritize the target behaviors.

15(a). Choose only one or two from your list.

15(b). Use other instructional strategies for the remainder of these behaviors.

to self-regulate. By minimizing (or making less c⟨
tendencies of children whose behaviors and characte
autism, we may facilitate, if not maximize, their abil⟨
existing social situations. Using this approach first asks us
teachers, and therapists, to change our behavior, our app⟨   ⟩d
the learning environment. Only then can we go about changing
those of the children.

Social communication

The development of communication is one of the most empowering
skills a child with autism can learn. We know that communication is
more than speech. It is also more than language. It is the mutual
exchange and understanding of a shared set of symbols that allows us
to communicate with one another in social situations. When we
examine the nature of communication problems in children with
autism, we must consider not only their ability to acquire speech and
language (the symbols) but also their proficiency at exchanging this
information when they need to within a social context.

I could write this entire chapter with the exact same words in
another language, but if you were not proficient in reading this
language, I would fail in my attempt to communicate my message to
you because we do not share the same symbols of language. To
appreciate the gravity of the autistic child's disabled communication
system, it is helpful to accept these two tenets:

1. Assume nothing. Never assume that he or she is understanding all that you are saying to him or her. Therein lies the
   problem. You may be speaking but not communicating.

2. Regard every word as a "concept."

Teachers make requests every day that on the surface may seem
simple. "Put away your backpack and go to your seat" can actually be
broken down into at least six concepts that a child with autism must
decipher (*put away* + *your* + *backpack* + *go to* + *your* + *seat*). Successful

mpletion of this command first requires a child with autism to translate personal possessives, verbs, and a noun with multiple meanings; then to remember them in order to discern "where" to put the backpack from inference; and finally to comply. Why are we surprised then if the child with autism fails to follow this very complicated direction?

Nearly every parent of a young autistic child has asked the question "When will my child speak?" Paradoxically, nearly every parent of a (usually older) child with Asperger's syndrome has lamented "Will he ever stop?!" It is hard to believe that these two questions could be asked about children with the same condition. What the parents of each of these children are really saying is "When will he ever communicate?" Although the language impairment in autism surfaces in differing ways across the spectrum, the problem is always the same – this is a problem of functionality, of using the language in meaningful, practical, flexible, and social ways.

In a personal essay, Kathy Lissner states: "I didn't start talking until I was four – haven't stopped since. I learned how to talk when my dad rounded up all six kids and said, 'Spend 15 minutes a day with Kathy. I don't care what you do, just as long as it is 15 minutes a day.' Fifteen minutes may not seem like much, but multiply that by six, seven, ten, or 15 sessions, and you get 90, 105, 150 and 225 minutes" (1992, p.304).

Years ago, I acquired a text that was instrumental in helping me grasp the importance and the complexity of the development of speech. It strikes me as ironic that speech typically comes reliably and effortlessly in most young children, so much so that we easily take it for granted. In *The Speech Chain*, Denes and Pinson (1970) put into context the monumental importance of language: "The development of human civilization is made possible – to great extent – by man's ability to share experiences, to exchange ideas, and to transmit knowledge from one generation to another" (p.1). We have all probably had the pleasure of listening to a "good" speaker. Likewise, at some time, we have undoubtedly been in the presence of someone who is "very" social. I am sure the reverse of each of these situations is true as well. I strongly believe there is a strong correlation between one's level of socialness and communicativeness. Social people use communication to their advantage when relating to others. Those who have adroit communication skills are frequently successful socially. Sadly, children with autism, including those with Asperger's syndrome, have both strikes against them. This makes teaching them so difficult because we face a double barrier: we cannot use one to advance the skill level of the other:

> problems with language are not the only symptoms associated with autism, but they are the most noticeable, the most dramatic... The educational goal should be to be more communicative, not more verbal...adults should be careful not to confuse form with function. Many parents think [getting] better means more verbal. (Hart 1995, p.65)

As Hart suggests, helping children with autism to develop communication skills is more than speeding up a developmental delay in language or developing verbal skills. To do so would suggest that the nature of their problem is a linear one, and it is not. The autism condition is considerably more complex and therefore more difficult to remediate.

I have observed that children with autism can make the most rapid progress in verbal speech development during the years in early childhood, kindergarten, and sometimes through second grade. It seems there is a window of opportunity that we must seize, making early intervention an absolute. Every child is different, of course, and we should never give up on helping them to communicate, even in later years. However, at some point we must make a decision to shift gear from a verbal speech approach to alternative (or argumentative) language development. The techniques that follow are divided into sections based on speech ability. Some ideas certainly overlap. The lists are not meant to be mutually exclusive.

Developing language in young children with autism

1. Teach receptive before expressive skills: expect the child to demonstrate understanding by pointing, giving, matching, showing the desired item or picture.

2. Concentrate on establishing concrete linguistic concepts which are tangible.

3. Reinforce spontaneous attempts to communicate, even if they are only approximations.

4. Use a behavioralist approach when introducing novel concepts. Children with autism rarely acquire new or difficult language concepts unless they are introduced in structured, individualized lessons.

5. Parallel talking by teachers and therapists expands receptive vocabulary.

6. Develop a core vocabulary of high interest/high usage nouns, verbs, adjectives (qualities, shapes, colors, etc.). To check for comprehension, expect the child to use these vocabulary words in multiple ways, with different people and in varying contexts.

7. Introduce associated concepts (such as hot/cold) in completely separate presentations, work them into the same lesson only after the child has mastered each.

8. To encourage generalization, use the technique that I call "novel redundancy." Have the child demonstrate understanding or use a target vocabulary word given novel and varied stimuli.

9. Answering questions of a basic nature is critical at this age. As with other concepts, restrict activities to one question at a time, then gradually mix them. Generally, children are more successful beginning with "what?" and "who?," then

progressing to "where?". "Why?" and "how?" are always the most difficult.

10. Children who are prone to acting on impulse, who seem to have unpredictable behaviors, tend to favor using their bodies rather than their words. Take this opportunity to give them the language (verbal, sign, picture, etc.) to express themselves.

11. Eye contact is good for children with autism to have, but it is overrated. Years ago, I remember writing goals for my students whereby they would "make and sustain eye contact" for one or two minutes. When was the last time you made eye contact with anyone for two minutes in length? Try it sometime. Eye contact is necessary to help us communicate in social situations. Knowing when to look away is as important as knowing when to look.

Advancing the communication skills of verbal children on the autism spectrum

Teaching children to speak in complete sentences is less important to me than having them use accurate, meaningful language. I am prone to accepting the spontaneous, three-word utterance if it is social in nature and if it makes sense in context.

Children on the higher end of the spectrum are masterful memorizers of facts, figures, and details. They should be challenged to develop and use higher order thinking skills, such as those on the upper level of Bloom's taxonomy (Bloom and Krathwohl 1976; see also Table 6.1).

If perseveration and topic fixation are problems, set a rule about how long, where, and with whom these discussions will occur. Encourage interest in variations and permutations of the favorite subject rather than a completely different subject. (For example, rather than dwell upon colonial history, branch off into other periods.)

When a child uses either immediate or delayed echolalia, this is actually a hopeful sign because it gives us something to work with. Delayed echoing patterns give us an insight not only into their interests, but also their memorization capabilities. View all echolalia as attempts to communicate. Immediate echolalia is easily dealt with by eliminating questions (which tend to be echoed rather than answered). If a child is prone to repeating what you say, teach him (through repetition) 50 to 100 new words. Gradually fade questions into the words that you know he knows spontaneously.

Answering yes/no questions is never easy for a child with autism. There are two categories of yes/no questions: affirmation/denial and expressing wants, needs, opinions. Because there is intrinsic motivation, it is advantageous to begin having them answer questions related to their desires. As with other dual concepts, you may meet with more success by teaching the yes response in repetitive fashion and in isolation from the no response. Using icons or head nods as cues is helpful. Mix questions that require a yes or a no response once you have established with certainty that they can discriminate what they want and do not want.

Despite having more advanced language skills, many children will confuse personal and possessive pronouns. Because he and she are gender related, they may be easier to teach than those that are socially oriented (I, you, my, your). Pairing words with pictures usually helps these children make the connection. But because these words go up a notch on the level of abstraction, they are difficult to teach.

Augmentative communication strategies for low verbal children

Many children on the autism spectrum struggle to express themselves. Not only do they fail to acquire verbal speech, but they also appear especially aloof and difficult to reach. It is rare to see them make a spontaneous effort to communicate. We must find a way to circumvent these problems and start their ability to initiate.

The Picture Exchange Communication System (PECS) developed by Bondy and Frost (1998) was revolutionary because it accompanied all of the above. PECS has opened an entire venue of communication opportunities through pictures and icons. Its emphasis on developing initiation skills makes it one of the effective strategies used with this population.

Technology has broadened both our capacity to communicate and the speed and efficiency with which we do it. There are now any number of augmentative devices available, with options that advance continually, making it more possible for low verbal children to communicate.

Sign language was introduced to children with autism almost three decades ago. Although its popularity has faded in the light of newer augmentative techniques, the use of gesture is still a viable option for many children. Many gestures are now universal communication symbols, requiring only the manual dexterity and imitation ability to use them successfully.

Developing the receptive language skills in a low verbal child is advantageous because it circumvents the entire oral language path. Having the children choose from any given number of items or pictures allows them a way to show us what they know, request, and feel.

Sensory integration

Children with autism are each a unique mixture of under-reactors and over-reactors when it comes to the senses. How many times have we heard a parent lament about the fact that their son will only wear sweat pants (usually a particular brand, but always with the labels/tags removed)? Jeans and pants with belts, buckles, zippers and hard-to-close buttons or snaps are not an option. We have also seen the child with her ear lobes folded upward and fingers pressing inward when she hears a certain bell, whistle or sound. The list goes on and on, but each speaks to the fact that autism skews the children's ability to process what they see, hear, taste, feel, and smell.

Hermelin and O'Connor's (1976) text was one of the first to document this aspect of autism:

> It is understandable that educators who thought that information about the outside world comes to us through our senses, have long held the view that our inability to "make sense" of the world may be due to our inability to receive, and organize the incoming sense data. (p.24)

Autistic children who have dysfunctional sensory systems face an extraordinary challenge because they are surrounded and bombarded by sensations that seem only to bother or tantalize them, or both. I believe that their inability to focus, their unpredictable behavior, and some of their unruly outbursts stem from sensory integration irregularities. If they have a co-existing problem in communication, their difficulties are even more pronounced.

Uta Frith (2003) characterizes autism as an enigma because autistic children can vacillate between extreme reactions without reason or explanation. They can be propelled and highly aroused by one sensation, yet calmed and mesmerized by a competing one: "Being touched triggered flight; it flipped my circuit breaker…many autistic children crave pressure stimulation even though they cannot tolerate being touched" (Grandin 1995, p.62).

Although they lack the social communication skills to navigate their world successfully, many children on the spectrum, like Temple Grandin, are ingenious in creating adaptations in their environment:

> I was one of those pressure seekers. When I was six, I would wrap myself up in blankets and get under sofa cushions, because the pressure was relaxing. I used to daydream for hours in elementary school about constructing a device that would apply pressure to my body. (Grandin 1995, pp.62–63)

Indeed that is exactly what she did. Temple's "Squeeze Machine" can be found on pages 69 and 70 of her book *Thinking in Pictures* (1995).

Having a sensory integration specialist available for consultation is extremely helpful to a classroom teacher. Although I am not professionally trained in this area, I hang around several folks who are. I have had the advantage of watching as they add a "sensory diet" to a teacher's daily lesson, and the results are nothing but rewarding. Here are just some of their ideas.

Assessment

A sensory integration specialist can help to identify the level of involvement for each of the major senses. The range of involvement falls, by degrees, into four general categories:

- missing completely
- poorly organized
- under-developed
- over-developed.

A sensory diet consists either of a series of pre-planned activities throughout the school day to prevent or stimulate certain reactions, or it can be a series of options which can be used when a child behaves in a certain manner. It is important to consider the challenge level, the interest level, and the productivity level of each child when developing a sensory diet.

Alerting sensations are used to stimulate an under-reactive child, to reward a child who craves these sensations, or to focus a child who is poorly organized:

- brightness of lights and colors, contrasts, vivid patterns
- fast/quick movement
- loudness, rhythm or pattern of sound with emphasized features
- unexpectedness of approach, element of surprise, quick and changing events/sensations
- adjustment to level of physical or cognitive challenge (increase if bored, decrease if confused).

These strategies can find their way into any of the senses. They are effective in countering children who are slow to respond, difficult to reach, or bored with the status quo.

Calming sensations are used to manage a child who is overly active, physically difficult to manage, poorly organized, or who has adverse reactions to change or transitions:

- rhythmic, repetitive music or sounds (ocean music, haunting, instrumentals)
- dimness of lights, sounds, and speech
- gentleness and slowness of movement, touch, and speech
- predictability of events and consequences
- quiet, isolated time periods (headphones are helpful)
- desensitize by gradually fading in a sensory experience to which they are adverse (allow touching or smelling foods before tasting them)
- substitution of one sensation over another (use visuals rather than an auditory means of communication)
- use of repetitive vestibular and/or tactile sensations (rolling, rocking, deep pressure, massage, wrapping, brushing, stroking, swinging)
- use of heavy and resistive work – carrying, moving, stacking, organizing, pushing, pulling.

A room which uses sensory integration strategies has characteristics which make it unique in its appearance. Vestibular swings, weighted vests/blankets, lofts/alcoves, ball pits or tents, compression balls of various sizes, and body socks are common pieces of equipment. Additionally, there are alternative forms of lighting and music options available.

CHAPTER 5

Planning Strategies

> The one treatment for autism that has stood the test of time, and is effective for all children, is a structured, educational program geared to a person's developmental level of functioning. (Freeman 1993, p.19)

Over the past 25 years, I have observed hundreds of teachers. I have learned from watching them that the most successful are those who are structured and organized, and who plan ahead. By successful, I mean there is clear engagement and motivation of students with fewer behavioral outbursts, increased time on task, individualization, and finally accountability for student performance. I have also seen that the best laid plans can go awry. Students with autism can unpredictable and demanding, creating intense need for structure and consistency. I have come to realize that the teachers who fail to put time into planning, curriculum, and organization are the ones who have problems staying on top of things. I tend to see more behavioral and attentional problems in the students who are in these classrooms. Poor planning and organization only make the job more difficult, and that is the last thing we want for teachers.

Lesson plans

Once the Individual Education Plan (IEP) is written, planning becomes a feature of mapping out incremental steps to this end. An

entire (other) book could be written to outline the proper development of IEPs for kids on the autism spectrum. This text assumes that
the reader is satisfied that the student's IEP is appropriate. This being
said, the section now discusses the strategies one should use in
developing daily (or short-term) lessons.

Teachers have to be visionaries who live and work in the
moment, but who can see into the future. That statement may seem
contradictory. In training in-services, I always see concern on the
faces of my audience when I tell them they must be structured but
flexible, organized ahead of time, but ready to be creative when
necessary. But that is the whole essence of this art and science model.
There is no one technique, method, or prepared plan for how to do
this job successfully. I have always felt that teaching is "theatre" – it's
an art – you have to know your lines, where your mark is, and don the
right costume. But you also have to play to your audience when the
time comes, adding emphasis or adlibbing your lines when necessary.
What follows are suggestions for planning effective instructional
activities.

Thematic instruction

This is not a new technique but it has always been one of my
favorites. You often see themes, or units, in pre-school and kindergarten classrooms. Susan Kovalik and Karen Olsen (1993, 1997)
have in-depth suggestions on this topic and they are worth review-
ing. But I think thematic instruction makes sense for students with
autism at any age. Rather than isolate the domains of reading,
spelling, math, writing, etc., thematic teaching merges all of these
activities around a central idea.

Children with autism are pretty good at learning in isolation.
However, they are especially challenged when asked to transfer
(generalize) this knowledge to new situations, with new people, in
different contexts. Thematic instruction is a planning strategy that
ameliorates this dilemma from the outset. It is an approach that

emphasizes purpose and function in the skills we typically teach children.

Some teachers may prefer two or three mini units over one large one. This is advantageous because those mini units can build upon one another. I was recently talking with a teacher who was experiencing difficulty in having her first grade age students (with autism) understand sound–letter relationships. While some made the connection, they failed to apply it. Others were confused because the idea was too abstract. The students were diverse in their energy levels and interests, and it was hard to get them all to stay focused. We decided that she should try to introduce a mini-unit approach. Phonics was one of the themes, but we restricted it to only five consonants. Next she chose machines because one student was fond of VCRs, and finally, she chose animals, as this was developmentally appropriate. She set her sight for one week, whereby the majority of her core subjects were taught within the context of one of these units. The next set of themes included five more consonants, transportation and the color green.

The Premack Principle

The influence of David Premack (1959, 1961; Premack and Collier 1962) spans across many disciplines and several decades, culminating in his most recently published text, *Original Intelligence* (2003). As a result of his studies on motivation and reinforcement, he became noted for the strategy which bears his name. Many of us have used the Premack Principle in our planning of lessons for teaching children with autism. Essentially, he taught us that a low-probability behavior (one that is disliked or not preferred) will be more willingly performed if it is followed by a preferred (or liked activity). If you reflect upon any child with autism, you will probably see that his or her preferred behaviors are the ones engaged in with great frequency, but are not the ones that we would ask that he or she engage in. Examples of this may be self-stimulating actions, perseverative interests, out-of-seat behavior, etc. Using Premack's idea, I have seen teachers become very successful in instruction if they plan to follow a disliked activity with a liked activity. It is a non-traditional sequence, that's for sure, but it works with astonishing ease. Successful use of this strategy involves a lesson plan that follows a L–D–L–D series through the day. The nature of the preferred and non-preferred activities is highly variable between classrooms. For some, snack is "liked," while for others eating is a chore – so it is switched to "disliked" status.

Tables 5.1 and 5.2 are examples of two daily activity plans over two weeks – one for younger children, the other for older students with Asperger's syndrome.

Table 5.1 Pre-school schedule

Week 1	Week 2
D 9:00–9:10 Calendar	D 9:00–9:20 Calendar
L 9:10–9:30 Scooter Boards	L 9:20–9:30 Scooter Boards
D 9:30–9:40 Numbers	D 9:30–9:50 Numbers
L 9:40–10:00 Bubbles	L 9:50–10:00 Squirt Guns
D 10:00–10:10 Sorting	D 10:00–10:20 Categorizing
L 10:10–10:30 Snack	L 10:20–10:30 Snack
D 10:30–10:40 Story Book	D 10:30–10:50 Story Book
L 10:40–11:00 Balls	L 10:50–11:00 Mini-Tramp
D 11:00–11:10 Tracing	D 11:00–11:20 Tracing
L 11:10–11:30 PlayDoh	L 11:20–11:30 Coloring Books

(L=like, D=dislike)

Week One and Week Two have similarities, but also differences. With the younger children, keeping many of the activities constant is important for developing their organizational abilities. However, the length of time spent on the various activities changed (and should continue to change) over time with them spending more time on disliked activities and less on preferred ones. The junior high students' schedule is similarly age appropriate, but differing markedly in the length of activities. Week Two breaks the non-preferred time into two activities, but the overall duration is increased. Of all the strategies I've used, the Premack Principle has been the most effective one, and it is invaluable as a tool for teachers of students who have autism.

Table 5.2 Junior high schedule

Week 1	Week 2
D 9:00–9:30 Geometry	D 9:00–9:20 Vocabulary
L 9:30–9:40 Jigsaw Puzzles	D 9:20–9:45 Power Writing
D 9:40–10:00 Literature	L 9:45–10:00 Board Games
L 10:00–10:10 Game Boy	D 10:00–10:30 Pre-Algebra
D 10:10–10:30 English	D 10:30–10:45 Social Studies
L 10:30–10:40 Choice	L 10:45–11:00 Recess
D 10:40–11:00 Analogies	D 11:00–11:10 Music Education
L 11:00–11:10 Recess	D 11:10–11:30 Diagraming

(L=liked, D=disliked)

High demand–low demand times

With a few exceptions, most of us function more efficiently in the morning. This is the time when, all things being equal, we are at our best. When planning lessons for students who have autism, it is advantageous to know when they are apt to respond the best, because one can arrange lessons (demands) accordingly. If indeed mornings are when students are at their optimum, then schedule the hardest activities first. Arrange less demanding activities for the latter part of the day. If concentration and attention span are issues during a disliked activity, it is recommended that a given time period be broken down into two or three related but different demands. Rather than ask that students compute addition facts for 20 minutes, ask that they do three math-related activities in different areas of the room such as:

1.   Addition facts to 100 – desk, seated.

2.   Sort odd versus even numbers to 100 – floor, sitting.

3.   Add > or < to number sets – wall mural, standing.

Every group of students is different, but we can maximize their learning by matching our demands to their ability and effort levels.

Curriculum

If I could produce a curriculum for teaching children with autism, I bet I'd sell a whole lot of copies. I have been asked, time and again, what type of curriculum I use. I think this is such a puzzle to people because they are already aware that autism runs its course in individual and unpredictable ways across the spectrum. Usually when teachers ask this question I realize they are trying to work around splinter skills, that quirky uneven development that many autistic children have. Their learning rate and learning style also complicate this situation.

It is hard to predict with any degree of certainty where a child will be one, two or three years on. That is why an IEP team should put considerable effort into calculating a child's goals and objectives, for this is essentially his or her curriculum. Learning theory and curriculum have an odd relationship. Sometimes they are in synchrony with one another and seem to co-exist peacefully. At other times, they seem to move in opposite directions. In 1984, when Benjamin Bloom developed the taxonomy of learning objectives, he was respectfully observant of the teaching process of curriculum. Bloom's theory about thinking and questions which teachers should ask is, in my opinion, highly pertinent to the instruction of children with autism. The issues he considered useful to us as we develop a curriculum for a child with autism include:

1. How much knowledge is required?

2. How precisely [should] the student learn [this] knowledge?

3. How is knowledge best organized for learning?

4. How meaningful is this knowledge to the student?

(Bloom and Krathwohl 1976, p.36)

Bloom's hierarchy of questions can be found in Table 6.1.

Learning theory and curriculum have an odd relationship. In some classrooms, they are in synchrony with one another; in others, they seem to peacefully co-exist. Still in others, they seem to move in opposite directions. I would like to suggest that teachers must use both (learning theory and curriculum) together, in order to be successful in developing meaningful goals and objectives for children with autism. Benjamin Bloom's contribution to this partnership will be discussed in Chapter 6. However, it is important for teachers to anchor their lessons in alignment with his hierarchy of questions, as they develop a curriculum and learning sequence for children with autism.

Long-term outcome

Curriculum is a tool, a master plan if you will, that serves as a general guidepost for learning. It helps us (in education) to reach a given set of learning outcomes. Every school has a mission statement about what children should take away from their school experience. We should attempt to have our students with autism blend into this mission when and if this is possible. The more special support a child needs, however, the farther we move away from traditional instruction and curriculum. Many of our students will never be "on the same page at the same time" as their non-disabled peers. That may be disappointing to some, but I say that it is okay. We have a legal and moral responsibility to provide an appropriate education. Sometimes this means we must try alternative methods and formats in order to accomplish this. If a child can function in a regular education class and learn (given accommodations and modifications), then she or he should be given this opportunity.

Textbooks

The curriculum of students who cannot funtion in a regular education class must closely follow the goals and objectives of the IEP, and reflect standardized learning benchmarks as much as possible. Most students' learning needs are met through textbooks. Textbooks may only partially meet a student's needs. Frequently the scope and sequence of the textbook must be altered, repeated, and broken down into smaller increments. When this process is not efficient there are other curriculum options that may be more appropriate.

Hands-on learning experiences

One of the best ways to reach children with autism is through hands-on learning experiences because concepts are presented in a way that makes them more tangible and concrete Children learn by doing, and if they can see it, do it, watch it, manipulate it, they are .e prone to focus and learn what they need to learn. When planning, teachers are advised to use a hands-on activity to introduce a novel idea or abstract concept. One of the first questions we ask a student on Monday mornings is "How was your weekend?" This is not a simple question to answer because it involves two very complicated concepts: the first being an abstract temporal one (weekend), the second being an opinion (how?). Can you see a weekend? Can you feel it? If we want an answer, we must somehow bring tangible qualities and terminology to our request. A better way to approach this would be to use a "curriculum bridge," where we ask parents to inform us about significant events. A home–school bridge thus helps us with our question.

Task analysis

From the long-term goals and short-term objectives, we must further break down complex expectations into sequences of tasks. A task analysis is a hierarchy of steps from the most basic to the skill at mastery level. This technique has been used for many children with special needs, but it is especially helpful for students with autism. While it is important for us to know the sequence of a task such as recognizing numbers from 1 to 100, it is also critical for teachers to realize that learners with autism are frequently not sequential learners. In fact, they skip stages of development, and appear to have acquired a skill when they have only learned pieces of it. We should never assume that a child with good decoding skills actually understands the words or numerals that he or she has decoded. The task of recognizing numbers 1 to 100 is only one of a number of steps at mastering beginning mathematics. When we put this into the perspective of a task analysis of "mastery of math skills at the first grade level," it helps us to know where the child really stands.

Organization and structure

The physical properties and organization of a room for one (or more) students with autism is as important as the lesson plan. Sometimes it appears that these children are in chaos (organizationally, behaviorally, sensory processing, socially, and communicatively). I have found that there is a direct correlation between "disorganization" (of the classroom) and "behavioral" problems (of the students). Likewise, the reverse seems to be true. Children with autism cannot seem to regulate or control themselves, and they are dependent upon us to provide them with this control. Most people know an organized room when they see it, but just in case there is a question, here are the top ten features that I think make the most difference:

1. Clear pathways and boundaries (like roads) to guide traffic throughout the classroom.

2. Varied types of structured learning areas (desks, tables, chair groupings).

3. Areas for semi-structured "down time" or planned sensory experiences.

4. Activity schedule (class and individual).

5. Order and neatness in storage of materials and other classroom necessities for learning.

6. Use of size, color, contrast, and patterns of text, borders, and framery that accentuates/frames messages to students.

7. Centers (or areas) that reflect ongoing projects, themes, social stories which reflect student words, ideas, opinions, art projects, or other creations which demonstrate the use of the theory of the multiple intelligences.

8. Well-organized storage areas, minimal clutter, consistent use of space, where materials which are stored are out of the way to the extent possible.

9. Three-dimensional elements which enhance walls, floors, ceilings, as well as visually cued learning and activity areas and traffic patterns; activity schedules using icons, pictures, words, scripts, checklists, etc. which provide time orientation.

10. Wall displays that reflect an emphasis on literacy, social skills, and communications skills, which are organized and labeled accordingly.

CHAPTER 6

Instructional Strategies

Every student is a genius. (Armstrong 1998, p.1)

What we teach (curriculum) and how we teach (instructional process) are large-scale issues facing every teacher. This chapter addresses instructional methods that are useful with children who have autism. This is a broad statement, because methods will vary according to context, objective, and the student's level of autism. Instructional strategies can vary on a daily basis, or they might remain static for weeks. Teachers should adjust their teaching approach with the changes in student development (either progression, or lack thereof). Students on the spectrum will require at the very least modifications and adaptations in the pace and complexity of instruction. Other students may require highly specialized strategies and significant alterations in class size, unique methods, and supportive therapies.

Teaching to the multiple intelligences (MI)

Howard Gardner (1983, 1993, 1997, 1999) has been a catalyst in changing perceptions about how we determine who is smart. Gardner expanded the concept of intelligence not only in terms of its depth, but also in its scope. Gardner's investigations into authentic assessment led him to conclude there are many ways to be smart (in fact, he proposed seven). Gardner and his colleagues concluded that traditional, standardized assessment only examined two of these intelligences: logical–mathematics and linguistic. Children who were capable in these areas received higher IQ scores and were regarded as being more intelligent.

Questioning the fairness of this ultimately led Gardner to the theory of the multiple intelligences. From this emerged the instructional corollary that all children can progress if the teaching style matches their learning style, and when they are given opportunities to demonstrate their intelligence in productive ways in the classroom. It is interesting to note that Gardner himself referenced autism when explaining the variability between the intelligences within individuals themselves.

> Autistic people are an even clearer example, since many autistic children are outstanding at numerical calculation, musical performance or reproduction of melodies, or drawing. At the same time, they characteristically evince marked impairments in communication, language and sensitivity to others… Like the autistic person, prodigies tend to emerge in domains that are rule governed and that require little life experience. (Gardner 1999, p.39)

Gardner put his theories into practice when he established Project SUMIT and began to collect data from schools whose teachers used MI theory during instruction. His text *Intelligence Reframed* (1999) published these outcomes from 41 schools across the United States. Seventy-eight percent had positive outcomes on standardized tests (63% of these reported a correlation between improvement and the use of MI during instruction). Eighty-one percent reported improved student behavior (67% attributed this to MI theory [p.113]).

New City School in St. Louis, Missouri, has provided enormous inspiration to me for over a dozen years. Although their student population does not target children with autism, I have been struck by the creativity and consistency with which they use the theory of MI. Because New City welcomes visitors, I have conveniently used it as a haven at least once per year to really think about curriculum and

instruction. Long before I read any of Gardner's b
convinced after watching the activity at New City t'
multiple intelligence explained (very vividly) hov.
autism learn, and how we should teach them. I began to in...
this philosophy into practice when I trained or consulted wiu.
teachers. The teachers at Franklin School, where I am currently
based, integrate MI theory quite successfully for students with
autism. I am indebted to New City School, especially its Director,
Tom Hoerr, for serving as a sounding board for my ideas.

I attended New City School's Conference on Multiple Intelligences in 2002. I learned a lot, but I was most impressed with Tom
Hoerr's letter to the conference participants:

> MI has been good for our kids and good for our faculty. Simply
> put, our kids achieve due to MI... Our use of MI enables our
> teachers to become more than simply disseminators of knowledge; our teachers are artists weaving their curriculum tools
> into a fabric that helps our students grow and learn. (Hoerr
> 2002)

Gardner, Hoerr, and other supporters of the multiple intelligence
theory have shown us that there are gifts and genius in every child.
We can overlook these qualities, or we can cultivate them. There are
many ways to be smart, there are many ways to learn, and therefore,
there should be many venues of instruction.

Teaching children with autism can be overwhelming. It can also
be a triumph. Clara Park is the mother of Jessy, a gifted young
woman with autism who is also an artist. In an essay explaining her
daughter's strengths and weaknesses, she wrote: "If Jessy's painting
bespeak her handicap, it is a handicap not surmounted, but transmuted into something rich and strange. Here is autism in its core
characteristics, literal, repetitive, obsessively intact – yet beautiful"
(1992, p.253).

Box 6.1 offers a schema of MI theory as it can be applied to
students with autism. It puts their "smart" behaviors into context of
Gardner's seven intelligences, and it offers teaching techniques that
can enhance this intelligence.

Box 6.1 Multiple intelligences (MI) and teaching techniques

Logical–mathematical intelligence

Examples of ASD characteristics

- Learns symbols easily and manipulates them in operations.
- Follows sequential patterns.
- Proficient/interested in video games.
- Dismantles (and sometimes rebuilds) mechanisms, such as clocks, locks, computers, etc.
- Focuses on rules/hierarchies or other organizational elements.
- Demonstrates black and white reasoning.
- Has a strong sense of justice/right and wrong.
- Adheres to routine.
- Responds to consistency and predictability.
- "One-way" problem solver.
- Good-to-excellent rote memory for factual information and data.

Teaching suggestions

- Classroom should be orderly, well organized, areas labeled.
- Use color coding, font size, and contrast in patterns, sequences, hierarchies to depict relationships.
- Predict change in advance.
- Reinforce with manipulates with intricate interlocking components, multiple pieces, puzzles, etc.

- Develop "range" of problem solving by using color gradation or number/Likert scales to demonstrate levels of correctness, appropriateness, or applicability to a given problem.

- Encourage students to explain "why" they answered in a given way (regardless of the correctness or incorrectness of the answer). This is advantageous for two reasons: it gives teachers/therapists the rare opportunity to understand the students' behavior, and it demands that students reach into the abstract, beyond the realm of memorized answers, and create a rationale or justification for their answer. For children with autism, this is usually very difficult.

- To determine level of ability, expect identification of "wrong" answers (rather than "correct" ones).

- To broaden rigidity of any response, interest or item selection, expect use of two, three, then four selections, rather than one.

Linguistic intelligence

Examples of ASD characteristics

- Imitative ability, including echolalia.

- Memorization of words and phrases including topic fixation and perseveration.

- Unusually developed vocabulary.

- Pedantic, "quaint" speech quality.

- Proficient in decoding words by phonetic elements.

- Ability to use pictures, icons, or other graphics for communicative purposes.

- Preference for advanced or adult-level word use.

Teaching suggestions

- Use scripts, stories to broaden use of language beyond rigid boundaries.

- Offer opportunities to converse with older/advanced role models.

- Use written words, checklists to give multiple directions.

- Broaden ability to see similarities and differences in vocabulary, word structure and meaning.

- Introduce concepts at a concrete level, then move to more abstract ones.

- Teach ability to discriminate – ask contrasting questions, ask to compare/contrast two or three given items, events, concepts.

- Add graphics, icons, and other non-verbal cues to the instructional process and to items in the environment.

Intrapersonal and interpersonal intelligences

Examples of ASD characteristics

- Relates to "impersonal" qualities of others (your license plate number, phone number, the date/location you first met, your weight, hair color, other physical characteristics).

- Uses pre-scripted phrases in social situations.

- Strong adherence to predicted sequences of social events.

- Preference for non-human contact during social outings.

- "Independent" at an early age.

- Regards people as objects, barriers, or facilitators rather than friends.

Teaching suggestions

- Practice social-pragmatic language strategies for use in conversations with others before they occur (initiating, interrupting, concluding, repairing, inferring, etc.).

- Develop perceptual ability to discern para-linguistic messages sent through facial expressions, body language, proximity, and gesture.

- Allow "non-human" time during social outings and incrementally decrease it.

- Allow choices for social outings, contacts, and conversations.

- Encourage relationships with acceptable younger or older persons if same-age peers are difficult.

- Predict one, then two, then three changes in a comfortable social routine (use visuals, sequence strips, etc. to ensure understanding).

- Give pre-scripted words or non-verbal signals to communicate need for isolation, regrouping, de-escalation.

- Establish understanding of "concrete" expectations for various types of communication: listening, collaborating, arguing, conversing, etc.

- Encourage opinions.

Visual–spatial intelligence

Examples of ASD characteristics

- Strong preference for noting visual elements.

- Appears to be "visually distractible."

- Answers without looking (or seeming to have paid attention).

- Sees visual relationships (rather than social relationships) between items, words, persons, locations, events.

- Orientation to maps, graphs, tables, diagrams, borders, visual contrasts.

- Remembers locations with precision, or after only casual exposure.

- Proficient at puzzles, mazes, figure–ground identification, codes, three-dimensional representations.
- Non-verbal ability exceeds verbal ability.
- Extreme attention to detail.
- Reproduces pictures or other visual stimuli with astonishing accuracy.
- Can decipher information/reproduce information backwards or upside down.

Teaching strategies

- Display visuals that reflect student curriculum, work, projects.
- Use puzzles, mazes, and other visually oriented activities as reinforcement for completion of more challenging activities.
- Use color, contrast, borders, etc. to present new information or to structure expectations and responses.
- Present a difficult concept (or idea) non-verbally before expecting the child to verbalize it. One might request that the student "point to," "match," "show," or "find" an item (word, picture, or action) prior to asking him to identify it. Speech/language pathologists refer to this technique as teaching receptive recognition of a concept prior to its expressive state.
- Use visual organizational tools (e.g. table of contents, pre-written sentences, diagraming, webbing) to depict complicated or abstract relationships between concepts or situations.
- Work toward assimilation of meaning and conclusion of visual information and facts, such as interpreting graphs, predicting from given facts, etc.
- Use visuals to depict social relationships and activities.

- Bring three-dimensional qualities to the room by adding lofts, alcoves, ceiling/wall displays.

Musical intelligence

Examples of ASD characteristics

- Fascination with musical qualities and patterns of videos, TV shows, radio jingles, advertisements.
- Noticeable positive change in attention and cooperation when music is used.
- Automaticity of speech is improved when music is used.
- Exact replication of pitch, cadence, rhythm for certain musical pieces or instruments.
- Music appears to calm and decelerate overly active, difficult-to-manage children.
- Strong association between words and melodies.
- Sing-song quality to speech (few intelligible words, but a recognizable melody).

Teaching strategies

- Use music to promote social interactions.
- Establish musical "cues" (cadence, melodies, rhythms, etc.) to indicate transitions and introduce new activities.
- Use music as a reinforcer.
- Sing while teaching.
- Use background instrumental music or repetitive chanting to set the mood/style of an activity.
- Use music to elicit and expand language/memory (e.g. fill in the blank, repeat a phrase or a chorus, etc.).
- Use new words with familiar melodies to complement a lesson in other areas.

- Use music to pattern movements in children who are awkward or less physically inclined.

Body–tactile–kinesthetic intelligence

Examples of ASD characteristics

- Moves with ease, agility, balance, and coordination.
- Moves around a lot, rarely in seat, climbing and jumping.
- Preference for inappropriate smelling, touching, tasting of people and objects.
- Strong food preferences and distastes.
- Unique-to-idiosyncratic movements, mannerisms, position in space.
- Strong tactile preferences and dislikes.
- Over- or under-seekers of sensory stimuli.
- Pica behavior, or "mouthing" and chewing of non-edible items.
- High pain tolerance.
- Prefers to use body rather than words.
- Distressed by many sensory experiences (some obvious, others not detectable).

Teaching techniques

- Desensitize the sensory experiences that are least tolerated using a gradual "shaping" procedure.
- Use vestibular and other large movement experiences as a reward, or as a de-escalation activity.
- Build in a lot of "movement" to instruction (move furniture and equipment, vary seating arrangements, allow walking or running whenever possible).
- Offer a variety of non-edible chew toys at certain times of the day.

- Give clear expectations of where to sit or stand, how t‹ get from point A to point B.

- Represent time intervals with auditory cues like timers, bells, whistles.

- Give "manipulatives" to keep a child busy, listening, or attending during long wait periods.

- Alter adverse sensory experiences (e.g. change time in hallways, cafeteria, or gym if auditory stimuli are not easily tolerated).

Developing problem solving and critical thinking skills

Bloom's taxonomy and higher order thinking skills

Benjamin Bloom (Bloom and Krathwohl 1976) took learning to another level when he developed a hierarchy of questions and a corresponding taxonomy of thinking and problem-solving skills. His text, *Taxonomy of Educational Objectives* (1976), establishes the need for asking the "right" (or "critical") questions. Bloom suggests a level of questions which increase in complexity and correspond to advances in levels of thinking in child development. In my opinion, Bloom's hierarchy is essential during the instructional process of children with autism. They help us to extend children's reasoning skills beyond the rote memorization of facts, or as Bloom would say, beyond the knowledge level, to comparing/contrasting, and to synthesis of information. Bloom's theory is relatively easy to use because it immediately imposes a structure for why and when we should ask certain types (levels) of questions. Table 6.1 illustrates the taxonomy from simple to most complex.

Bloom challenged us to change our questioning process to better fit the instructional level of our students. There should be a direct correlation between what we ask and our students' answers. Do teachers ask the "right" questions? If so, how can instruction be arranged to allow children to demonstrate what they know? Kathy

Table 6.1 Bloom's taxonomy and hierarchy of questions

Level of question	Level of thinking
Knowledge	Recall of facts and terms; systems of classification, organization, or categories; universal truths, theories, common ideas.
Comprehension	Literal interpretation of a question, to a higher level or to a new context, interpretation from part to whole, discarding irrelevant and unimportant facts, drawing basic conclusions, interpreting meaning, predicting.
Application	Transference of ideas to new situations in a different context, presenting a newly acquired word or idea, varying its presentation from the way it was originally introduced, moving away from an original concept to a new application or meaning.
*Analysis	Determination of how parts integrate and function as a whole, examining the organization of ideas, determining relationships and their level of arrangement within a broader idea.
*Synthesis	Putting elements together in a new way to form a new construct, clearing a new organization of existing data, seeing abstract relationships above original ideas, creating a new, original idea from previous constructs, creating broader outcomes.
*Evaluation	Drawing conclusions, judgements, offering opinions relative to the value of a new idea, hypothesizing about a new idea relative to economy, feasibility, and outcome – accumulation of all previous levels of questions/thinking.

Note: * indicates higher order thinking processes.

Lissner, a young woman with autism, is insightful about the importance of asking the right questions: "I often take things literally. Someone once asked me, 'Where are you?' and I said, 'Massachusetts.' She said, 'What do you want most out of life?' and I said, 'A hamburger.'" (1992, p.306).

For practical purposes, teachers should be aware of the types of questions they ask, the developmental level of the students who are to respond to a given question, and the corresponding level of instruction necessary to make it happen. A question used at the "knowledge" level might be "What is the population of Florida?" or "What is this girl doing?" At the comprehension level, one might ask "What comes next in this sequence: 10, 20, 30, 40, _____?" or "John is crying. He just saw _____?" In application, one might inquire after mastering the value of coins and bills, "What is your change at McDonald's if you give the cashier $5.00 and your purchase is $3.16?" Entering the higher order thinking phase requires creativity and generalization at the same time. This is extremely difficult for students with autism, and we should take great care to instruct them at this level. Asking them to analyze and answer a corresponding question might find a teacher asking "How are a dog and a wolf similar but different?" To many third graders, this would be a challenging, but fun question. A person with autism must be able to process the key words (dog, wolf, and similar, different). No doubt, they can tell us the name of each (knowledge level), but noting similarities and then differences may be more than they can handle. We must adjust our instruction accordingly, slowing down the process whereby we dwell for considerable time on the characteristics of both animals. We may use several of the ideas set out in Box 6.1 (e.g., webbing, diagramming, graphing, charting, color coding, font size, etc.) to get the point across relative to comparisons and differences. The answer to this (seemingly) very basic, obvious question may take weeks, not minutes. As Robert Sylwester notes in his text *A Celebration of Neurons* (1995), "Knowing why generally leads to knowing how" (p.5). In the case of a child with autism, this is a painstaking process. "Why" a child with autism says what he says, or does what she does, may never reveal itself. It is in this absence of an obvious, causal explanation for their behavior that we must construct a method to circumvent this mystery. We may never know "why," but we may come to realize "how" they learn.

Assimilating information, synthesizing ideas, and formulating conclusions are a feature of the highest in the order of questioning and thinking skills. My training, observations, and research have led me to believe that this step of the instructional process is one of the most critical. Teachers must be highly creative in arranging an environment (or learning circumstances) whereby these higher, more abstract questions can be formulated, discussed, and answered. Reflecting upon what this situation should look like, I realized that this meant the arrangement of a time and place for more active learning, where children are more participatory, where teachers ask what Grant Wiggins (1989, 1993) terms "essential questions." Wiggins and his colleagues have propelled school reform for over a decade in the United States in the area of assessment and in the instructional process, particularly in the area of constructing proper questions and inquiries to better engage students. Wiggins' model is supported by the Coalition of Essential Schools, an academic think tank located at Brown University in Rhode Island. Wiggins, a modern-day Bloom if you will, believes that students will comprehend and use knowledge in a more efficient, applicable manner if they are asked the appropriate questions. Classrooms with teachers who are trained to use this approach will appear very different to standard ones. I believe this trend is highly applicable to the instruction of children in special education, particularly those with autism. This instructional paradigm is especially appealing because it stretches the social/communication skills of its students. Reflecting upon what this situation should look like, I believe that this means asking teachers to arrange a time and a place for more "active learning." In this model, children become more participatory in the learning process. Although this is a departure from traditional instruction, I believe this theory should be a part of every teacher's curriculum, especially if they have students who struggle with interpreting language, such as those with autism, and who almost always fail to generalize or comprehend what information we teach them. Teachers who are aware of and ask the "essential questions" actually ask the "right" questions of children with autism. This method is compelling because it goes straight to the heart of the problems that plague children with autism every day. The following scenarios would be found in a classroom using Wiggins' approach:

1. The interaction between teachers and students is less dogmatic, where students are relegated to passive learning and listening, rather than participating and sharing in class discussions.

2. The teacher's goal for her students reaches beyond the memorization of facts. By asking her students essential questions, a teacher more readily engages them in active discussions.

3. Students are asked to research and to participate in collaborative problem-solving exercises rather than to read and record unified answers.

4. Teachers who use this approach routinely accept a range of correct answers, setting up open-ended inquiries and avoiding forced-choice questions.

5. Activities that are common to these types of classrooms are busy, interactive, and dominated by student voices, not the teacher's.

6. Students strive to answer why, to explain, to create, to compare/contrast, and to summarize material that they have learned about.

7. Teachers honor diverse opinions, new ideas, and creative solutions.

This is an important juncture for teachers of children with autism to understand. It is a departure from traditional instruction, but very useful because it works in a (dual) way to develop not only higher order thinking skills, but also social communication abilities (the intrapersonal and interpersonal intelligences).

JDT Resource Center (online 2003) offers a user-friendly
ective questions that would be good starters for teachers
to this technique. Some of their ideas include the following:

1. Ask students to seek evidence.

2. Ask them to explain.

3. Ask questions that relate to ideas, opinions, and theories.

4. Ask students to predict.

5. Minimize asking questions that have a simple yes/no answer.

6. Minimize teacher-dominated discussions.

7. Maximize asking students to elaborate.

8. Maximize the opportunity for students to ask the questions.

9. Maximize the time you allow for students to answer questions.

10. Use guide words like "why," "explain," "create," "compare and contrast."

Using the theory of constructivism and the project method

Everyone probably has fond memories of their kindergarten experience. (I didn't at first, because I missed my mom so much that I cried the whole time.) Why is this? Because kindergarten was fun. Think about it. You were always exploring, creating, talking out loud, touching and using things you usually weren't allowed to touch. I'd like to suggest that we return to this model when we instruct students who have autism. We spend a lot of our time encouraging them to sit down, pay attention, and to conform with group expectations. If we changed these group expectations, if only for a portion of the day, what might we find?

The method that I am suggesting, which kindergarten teachers put to such good use, is the "constructivist" theory of learning, initially defined by Kilpatrick (1918), advanced by Jerome Bruner

(1966, 1983), and popularized by Maria Montessori (1964, 1967, 1972). The Project Method, suggested by Katz and Chard (1998), is a more recent version of the original theory. While this method has typically been used with very young children, I feel it is very worthwhile for use by teachers of children with autism, no matter what their age (the children's age, of course).

Rarely in society will people function in isolation – not socially, and not cognitively. We will always need others to assist us, support us, teach us, no matter what our age or our role in society. Helping children with autism to learn the value of other persons is a critical life skill for them, because by their very nature they are contented isolates. The constructivist learning method is a useful means to this end. It dovetails nicely with the other theories discussed so far in this chapter because it facilitates them. This is a "hands-on" approach that allows many of their strengths (the body-kinesthetic, spatial, visual intelligences) to provoke development of their weaknesses (linguistic, and social personal intelligences). It sets the stage for developing higher order thinking by asking those critical, essential questions. In short, it is a theory of learning that teachers can rely on to develop those areas that children with autism so often struggle with.

The Project Method (constructivism) should focus around a problem, issue, or area of interest that is meaningful to the children you are teaching. This establishes a built-in motivational element from the beginning which will keep them engaged. Because this is an active process, there can be allowances for movement and discussion, so this is appealing to your overly active kids. Because projects are open ended by their nature, they can be as long or as short as a teacher determines. The Project Method allows deviation from textbook learning sequences. This is helpful when you have students with significant splinter skills, or who are developmentally diverse. Individual needs can be met by giving children a different role in the learning "project." This method is especially helpful to use in a classroom with young children with autism because it sets up additional opportunities for a child to use his or her social language skills. The process of a project involves the following steps:

1. Identification, as a group, of a mutual interest, problem, or issue for exploration.

2. Assignment of roles and experiences (researcher, field trips, surveyor, note taker, writer, proofreader, organizer).

3. Establishment of time lines for the project and for each person's assignment.

4. Allotment for group meetings for sharing, debate, discussion, and adjustment of project.

5. Identification of culminating experience of project outcome (group presentation, diorama, or other constructed displays, videotape, booklets, etc.).

6. Reflection component where higher order thinking questions are addressed (see Box 6.2).

Topics for projects are highly variable and unique to each group. This strategy is complementary to thematic teaching because it draws upon many domains (writing, reading, vocabulary, math, science, social studies). Developing higher order thinking and problem-solving skills are features of what Fennimore and Tinzmann (1990) term a "thinking curriculum." These strategies accelerate a child's potential in ways that other techniques we have discussed cannot. As John Dewey emphasized in his text *How We Think*, "learning is learning to think... Information is an undigested burden unless it is understood...it is knowledge only as its material is comprehended" (1998b, p.78).

Classroom tempo and style

If there is any method that requires a hefty dose of artistry, it is the tempo of a classroom, especially for students with autism. Unfortunately, it is one of the most difficult to portray in a book. The best way to explain it is to go back to how we recognize a child with autism. We now have pretty sophisticated checklists and diagnostic protocols for guidance in recognizing the autism spectrum disorders. However, the other side of that coin is knowing that we must rely upon our (own or someone else's) intuitive clinical observation to do so. Very experienced individuals can spot an autistic child in a waiting room or in a crowd of hundreds. That is not to trivialize the importance of a formal diagnosis, but there is that certain look, that unique mannerism, that style of behavior that is so often readily apparent, and one can quickly sense autism. This is the same sense you will get when it comes to recognizing the effectiveness of an instructional program. There is a sense that this is just right, and this sense almost always begins and ends with the teacher.

Box 6.2 Productive projects using constructivist learning theory

Ten questions which lead to productive projects using the constructivist learning theory:

1. Why was this project (issue, problem) chosen?

2. Compare/contrast this project with _____.

3. What steps were used in this project?

4. What happened as a result of this project?

5. What was your favorite part? Why?

6. What was your role in this project?

7. What do you know now that you didn't know before?

8. What part of the project was not necessary? Why?

9. Which partner will you want to work with again? Why?

10. What will you explore next?

I have been in hundreds of classrooms, and talked with that many (or more) teachers and parents. No matter what the presentation or philosophy of the classroom, it is the teacher that makes the difference. When you see him or her in action, you will know that he or she is good. As subjective as that word is, it is the truth, and we all know it. I have spent a lot of time trying to objectivity and qualify this term. If I could bottle it, it would be a big seller just like that curriculum idea.

I have been at numerous IEP meetings where a child is about to transition to a new program or a new classroom, and the discussion always comes back to who the teacher will be. One may hear "He needs a class just like Mrs. So-and-So's." While I also hear requests for certain methods, I know that it is the style of the teacher that is at the heart of this issue, not the teacher him- or herself.

Parents and school districts need to recognize this and develop a dialogue that can address it. For while I know that individual teachers do make a difference, it is actually their style of teaching that affects some students more than others. So rather than identify a particular teacher, we must identify his or her style, and then go about finding a compatible fit with a given student. Here are some of the extrinsic features of style and tempo that may assist you in determining a good fit between a teacher and student.

Structured down time

Although it is true that most children with autism prefer aloneness to socialness, they usually need "structured" aloneness. Too often a well-intentioned (but mistaken) teacher has commissioned "play time" and wonders where it all went wrong when the child with autism becomes disruptive. We have already discussed the language barrier that exists, so be careful to use terms that mean the same thing to both you and the child. Although you may know what you mean, the term "play time" may not provide enough guidance, structure, and boundary for a child with autism. A teacher would be advised to set physical and visual parameters, with clear-cut expectations about how and what to do during down time. Add a timer or clock alarm to signal beginning and endings of this period. Avoid letting the child with autism wander. Every minute of his day requires structure because it is likely he cannot provide it for himself. Keep him busy all the time. For some children a 15-second wait may be five seconds too long. Give the child something to do while he or she is waiting (e.g., move chairs to snack table, hold a kush ball while in line for the bathroom). If you fail to give them something to do, they will find something – bet you won't like it!

Sense of timing

Children with autism have a distinctly unique sense of time even though they cannot "tell" time. Typically, they move to their own "internal" clock, and it can be quite difficult getting them in synchrony with ours. When we use phrases like "wait a minute," "just a second," "in a little while," "I'll be right there," "it's not time yet," we impart a subliminal message about time that they will probably fail to comprehend. Likewise, on a larger scale, our social conversations and instructional expectations are laced with other rather abstract temporal conditions. My favorite example to make this point is "weekend" (as in "What did you do over the weekend?" What does this mean? Did you stand over a thing called a weekend and do something above it?). Even more common is the question "What month is it?" The understanding of the months of the year are difficult for children with autism to grasp because they are so abstract, and have conceptual underpinnings related to language and social aptitudes. We would be more successful instructing them about such things as "January" or "April" if we could somehow bring these abstract ideas to their level of understanding. Often this means making associations to concepts they already grasp, or by putting things into terms which come easier to them than language. Involving the sensations of touch, taste, smell, and/or motion into our explanation expedites their learning process and their comprehension. Helping them then to relate to what January might "feel" like, or what April might "smell" like is the key we need to be successful.

Eliminating those temporal conditions from our vocabulary is usually a good thing for the time being. See, I've done it to you, but you know what I mean when I say "for the time being." The important thing to know is that a teacher must be able to communicate time periods (or references to times of events) without relying on these typically used phrases. An effective teacher will represent time in highly concrete, tangible ways other than two hands and 12 numbers on a big circle. Tokens or tallies that can represent small increments of time are helpful. Timers with (pleasant sounding) buzzers are also effective. Activity schedules, posted and visible (individual or group), can be used to represent time periods as well as the passage of time.

Peak of interest

A companion strategy of the Premack Principle is peak of interest, and this technique rivals it in importance. Remember that students with autism appear to learn through (or make) associations. Sometimes they make associations we wish they wouldn't, and that is the driving importance of peak of interest.

How many times do we hear, or say, this child not only has autism, but he's hyperactive and he has an attention disorder? There is no doubt that children with autism are active and have problems focusing. We may never know if this child has the unfortunate combination of these three conditions or whether as a feature of autism he is active and cannot concentrate. It probably doesn't matter, but as teachers we must deal with these shifts in arousal and engagement. So even though you've got the best laid plans and you've done so according to the Premack Principle, you can run into problems with the children's unpredictability.

Being intuitively aware of their peak of interest in a given activity will help you manage them more effectively. The best (of the best) teachers that I have watched know how far and how long to keep an activity going. They know to change at the peak of interest because, by association, they prefer to have the student remember that he or she had a successful, cooperative, rewarding experience with a given activity. If time runs on, and a child is expected to remain past his "peak," the likelihood that he will become disruptive will increase. The teacher is then faced with regaining control rather than continuing with positive momentum.

It is to everyone's advantage then to know when there needs to be a shift in the schedule, maybe prior to what had been planned. A teacher who is a master at this technique is one who makes it look easy, not only because the students are engaged and focused, but also because she or he is a step ahead of them by watching for their peak of interest.

Equal opportunity to respond (EOR)

Within any given class, there is always a range of ability levels. Likewise there is a range of who naturally gets our attention and who does not. The principle of equal opportunity to respond (EOR) is in place to balance our attention. We are prone to gravitating toward dealing with interruptive behaviors. In doing so, we pass up an opportunity to reinforce and call upon that student who is holding it together. Sometimes this may be the lowest functioning child in the class, or it could be someone who has just mastered seat behavior and raising his or her hand. Remember that your attention is highly motivating. Remember that any behavior that received your attention (in any form) will most likely occur again. Use these techniques together to your advantage: reinforce students equally by giving them equal opportunity to participate.

Presentation

Madeline Hunter (1976, 1979) gave us a bonus when she developed her concept of instruction over two decades ago. These steps are important to find in any lesson, but for children with autism they are particularly helpful because they challenge us to be diagnostic while we teach a given lesson. I have found that the opening and closing segments are critical tools to keeping students with autism engaged. Opening an activity provides everyone with clear directives about what is expected. This is an especially useful tool when expectations must be individualized because it provides an automatic opportunity for giving students their assignments. Consequently, in closing, students are given a review of the activity. This reinforces sequential memory and serves as an opportunity to reinforce key language concepts. Finally, opening and closing a lesson gives yet another chance to ask higher level questions such as "What do you think will happen?," "Who will finish first and why?," "What was your favorite math concept today?"

Openings and closings are fairly easy to master and take only moments to accomplish. However, presentation involves other, more dynamic features that come intuitively to some, but must be modeled and rehearsed by others. When I began teaching many years ago, I had the opportunity to view myself on videotape. I had been trained (very well) to be objective, to use reinforcements, to be deliberate in the execution of operant conditioning principles, and this was obvious as the tape progressed. However, I was struck by what appeared to be a mechanistic, clinical, antiseptic approach. It bothered me then, and it haunts me now.

I spent a lot of time reflecting upon this observation. Somehow, within these thoughts I remembered another discussion I had had with some parents and teachers. From this I remembered someone saying "All he ever does is watch cartoons." Most children with autism love cartoons and videos. I'm sure many people have their hypotheses about why they are so fascinated by cartoons, but to me, at this time, I theorized that something about those cartoons held the key to their attention. Watch any cartoon and you'll see highly exaggerated color, sound, and action. You'll also hear staccato melodies and sound effects, as well as repetitive phrases, choruses, and theme songs.

That was all it took! I came to believe that teachers who emulated cartoon characteristics in their speech, action, and dress became captivating to children with autism. I will always believe there is merit to being objective and accountable, but I also know that a little drama and exaggeration can help the process along. When I observe teachers, I look for what I call a "snap-crackle-pop" tempo to their classroom. It is moving, moving, moving, but it makes great use of silence and anticipation. Teachers who use this technique combine an exquisite sense of timing, delivery, motivation, and suspense. If they have students who move at 100 mph, they move at 150 mph.

I believe this is why we see children who behave and attend selectively among various caregivers, teachers, and therapists. I believe in the power of a "commanding presence" for teachers. Visit a nearby discount store for a new magic wand, a bright colored baseball cap, a rubber duck prop, face glitter, and some oversized boots. One final note: there's only one situation worse than a child who is bored, and that's a child who is bored and who has autism.

Visually cued instruction

Visually cued instruction is one of the cornerstones of an effective program for students on the autism spectrum. Entire books can be found on the subject. Some of my favorites are Bondy and Frost (1994, 1998), Gray (1995), Hodgdon (1995), Quill (1995, 2000), but there are numerous others that are also worthwhile. In my opinion, there are but a few rare cases where a child on the autism spectrum will not benefit from visual cues and supports. It is clearly a best practice for this field, and any teacher who fails to use it only makes his or her job harder.

This is a time and labor intensive approach, so it is "costly" to use. Most of the techniques associated with visually cued instruction should be designed in advance. Having the support of program assistants (para-professionals) to help in the organization, creation, arrangement, and upkeep of a visually oriented classroom is of great benefit to teachers. In this way, they can better concentrate on the instructional process of their students. Here are some general areas that I have found to have tremendous benefit.

Visual schedules

Use visual schedules with children who have problems in these areas:

- following sequences
- understanding time concepts
- paying attention
- making transitions.

Visual schedules are also helpful in developing joint attention and for portraying the day's events in an organized way. Visual schedules can be individualized, small, and placed on one student's desk. They may also be quite large and on display for the entire group. Arrange the schedule vertically or horizontally, depending on how the student best understands a sequence of events. Schedule components can be removed as activities conclude if this assists students in understanding the process of completion. Activities can be portrayed by using words, graphics, icons, colors, and various font sizes or types. Velcro is useful for interchanging parts. Laminated strips can be re-used.

Visual boundary markers and traffic patterns

Use these aids with children who have problems in the following areas:

- getting from point A to point B

- losing their way and getting distracted
- difficulties understanding proximity between people or objects
- failing to understand basic environmental concepts (e.g., light, desk, calendar, art table, etc.).

Visual markers reduce the amount of verbal prompting required of staff and make students more independent. To establish success at any early stage, give students the matching word/icon or picture to carry to a given destination. Use color coded tape to map pathways, to designate boundaries, to cue seating and standing areas. Use color, or other emphasis, to indicate possessions or other items of importance.

Visual checklists

Use visual checklists with children who struggle in following multi-step directions, who have difficulty sequencing time and order of events, who are close to independent mastery of a complex task, or who must remember multiple "behavioral" expectations. A behavioral checklist should be with students wherever/whenever they are expected to comply with a set of expectations. It can be duplicated and given out whenever necessary, or it can be laminated for durability and remain with the student at all times.

Checklists can be posted at the location where a given task will occur (e.g., bathroom for a grooming checklist). A colored high-lighter can be used for removal of each step as it is completed. The steps of the checklist can be given at other times to allow the student to practice putting the sequence together. Icons, pictures, and color coding or other emphasis (e.g., for action words) will assists in comprehension.

Visual cues for choices

Use these visual cues with students who have problems in the following areas:

- difficulty answering yes/no questions

- difficulty making a choice from two or more options
- easily overwhelmed and may need a "break"
- rarely offer spontaneous answers
- difficulty understanding complex relationships between words (e.g., catagories, negation, classification, part-to-whole, etc.).

Visual cues can include icons, graphics, pictures, and color or font emphasis. Field of choice should begin small and work into larger numbers of options. Choices should begin at a student's desk and can work into a more distant graphic display at the board. The closer, simpler, and more graphic and fewer the choices, the more success the student will have.

Diagrams, webs, scales, and other visual organizers

Use with students who have a core vocabulary but need to learn more and advanced concepts and relationships, who need to develop higher order thinking skills such as giving more than one plausible answer, contrasting and comparing information, discarding un-necessary information, understanding a range of information, etc. Diagrams, outlines, webbing, scales, and other visual organizers give students a template for thinking and presentation of their ideas. These bring a level of concreteness to the process. Begin with partially completed visual organizers, or offer the students all of the information in individual pieces. Have them arrange accordingly. Students are at mastery level when they can choose the organizer that will fit a given assignment. Be rich with all of the visual cues such as graphics with color, size, contrast, patterns, pictures, icons, words, and phrases. Visuals which are most representational of the concept you are teaching are the most effective. The more abstract the picture or icon, the less meaningful it will be. Remember: maximize visual clues in every way. Auditory only presentations should be kept to a minimum.

Mastery learning

The rate at which a child learns is undoubtedly influenced by his or her innate capabilities. As John Carroll (1963) suggested, a student's aptitude is reflective of his or her learning rate. Carroll also reached the conclusion that every student is different, and that instruction should be adjusted accordingly if we expect all students to reach a designated outcome. Carroll's concept ultimately became known to us as "mastery learning." His ideas are especially useful to those who teach students with autism because we know that they present with great variations in rate of learning. As Carroll advised, if learning opportunities and the time allotted to them are adjusted for each individual, we can be optimistic that all children can learn.

Carroll's work influenced many of the learning and behavioralist theorists of the late 1960s, 1970s, and 1980s, and possibly the conceptual framework of the brain-based theorists in the 1990s. Mastery learning requires teachers to shift from group to individualized instruction so that all children can succeed. Mastery learning and applied behavior analysis are actually quite compatible strategies to one another. Teachers who use mastery learning take a broad end goal and divide it into a hierarchy of steps beginning with a task analysis of the skills and vocabulary needed at the outset. In a systematic way, the child moves from the most basic step through the final step, or mastery level of the skill. It is the sequence, timing, and execution of these steps that are critical:

1. Goals and objectives must be clearly defined on paper as well as in the classroom. Use observable, measurable terms: say what you mean, and mean what you say.

2. A task analysis should include all vocabulary, actions, and skills needed for the goal to be mastered. These must be isolated and taught before the lesson even begins. (A good task analysis may have 10 to 15 prerequisite skills. If there are more than that, the goal is probably inappropriate for the child at this time.)

3. The goal should be broken down into smaller units, each with a time frame for mastery. There may be daily, weekly, and monthly (or longer) expectations (units).

4. The child should be set up for success. Trial and error learning is not a component of mastery learning. Rather, children should be provided with "errorless" learning opportunities where they are given environmental supports. These supports can include (but should not be limited to) reduced field of choice, all levels and types of prompts, repetition of trials, use of tangible reinforcers, peer modeling, guided practice, and reteaching when necessary.

5. Criteria for mastery and informal assessment at each stage are important for determining the child's level of success. The instructional program and rate of instruction should be adjusted accordingly. The supports suggested above should be gradually faded as the child masters the goal.

6. Mastery learning can occur in most classrooms, not only in one-on-one situations. It does require extra time in planning and execution, and extra energy in order to ensure individually tailored instruction.

7. The time required for each mastery learning experience is individually determined by the aptitude of the student; therefore it varies in duration.

Mastery learning is useful because it is a technique that helps to equalize the playing field for students with diverse needs. Its reliance upon prompt hierarchies and curriculum modifications and adaptations is highly advantageous for learners with autism.

Naturalistic-incidental learning

We know that children with autism learn easily through association and operant conditioning principles (Lovaas 1969, 1977, 2000;

McEachin, Smith, and Lovaas 1993; Maurice 1993; Maurice, Green, and Fox 2001). However, applied behavior analysis (ABA) and its theoretical counterparts can only take a child so far on the continuum of learning. In recent decades, theorists have suggested that "naturalistic" or "incidental" instruction be used to establish generalization, comprehension, and maintenance of the skills acquired during the highly structured lessons used in ABA (Greenspan and Wieder 1997, 1998, 1999, 2000; Koegel and Koegel 1995; McGee, Krantz, and McClannahan 1986; Prizant and Wetherby 1998).

Essentially, in the course of naturalistic instruction the teachers and students switch places. Naturalistic instruction is child driven and occurs in real settings rather than in structured, adult-directed sessions. Instruction occurs incidentally, as the situation warrants it. Therapists seize on the opportunity as it presents itself. Play-based learning settings are optimum backdrops for this type of instruction. Children are encouraged to spontaneously apply what they know. Naturalistic-incidental instruction is less structured and less predictable. A child who requires structure and consistency will do poorly if this technique is used. Teachers can successfully use this technique:

- to expand knowledge of an already acquired base of information
- to generalize a learned concept from a structured environment to a new (unfamiliar) person, place, or presentation
- to maintain accuracy of knowledge over time by expecting use of a skill weeks or months after mastery
- to apply knowledge of a concept outside the context in which it was initially learned.

Children with autism struggle with the unpredictability of social-educational environments. Perhaps this is why they revert to memorized scripts and mantras. Naturalistic instruction is paramount to the success of any instructional program because it demands a level of generalization and comprehension not possible in discrete trial/ABA instruction.

Being flexible and responding spontaneously is the end goal of naturalistic instruction. Seizing an opportunity to have a child apply what he or she knows is the essence of incidental teaching. The following techniques reflect use of this theory:

1. Follow the child's lead. Provide learning and exploratory opportunities without directly imposing requests.

2. Accept partial responses that are spontaneous, though less than complete. Evaluate for usage (or understanding) of key concepts, actions, key vocabulary words.

3. Allow and encourage creative use of the above.

4. Ask open-ended questions rather than finite ones (e.g., "Tell me about this" versus "What is this?").

5. Use "parallel talk" to mirror what the child does (e.g., "You picked the blue fish…now he's swimming… Oh! He's out of the water…now you have the boat…"). This develops language capacity.

6. Encourage higher order thinking applications of concepts mastered in structured learning protocols (e.g., "Can you think of another way to use this? Where have you seen this [color, object, concept] before? How is _____ and _____ the same? What would you do if _____?").

Developing literacy

Literacy is a term that usually connotes reading mastery. However, I would like to expand this meaning to include mastery of language as well. As I see it, reading and language development are sister concepts on the continuum of communication. There is a facile relationship between the two because they both involve the exchange of ideas through a shared symbol set. Development of one or the other (either language or reading) is often compensatory because it facilitates understanding of the other.

Children with autism need both types of literacy, and we cannot afford to pass up an opportunity to develop both of them, preferably together. Because of their deep connection, reading and language instruction can be taught in parallel, reinforcing one another, and strengthening comprehension at the same time.

Most of the elements of language are found in reading, and vice versa, so merging the two processes is actually quite easy. Essentially language and reading mastery involve deciding, encoding, organization, and structure. But they also involve a higher order process called symbolism. Symbolism is inherently connected to higher order thought and social interpretation. Beyond teaching the mechanics of speaking, reading, and organizing thoughts, I feel there is strong support for helping students take what they have learned into a more abstract, social dimension. The continuum of literacy then begins with talking and reading, and moves to conceptualizing and understanding within a broader, social context. For students with autism, we must move across this continuum using their preferences to develop other aspects of literacy.

The mechanics of literacy

The development of speaking, reading, and writing begins with the merging and organization of the elements of speech, language, and graphics. Some students with autism are prolific decoders. They decipher the written word and discern meaning from other visuals (graphics, icons, etc.) without formal instruction. However, their ability to use this information to communicate is usually compromised. In order to develop the proper balance of encoding and decoding skills we must use their strengths (such as decoding) to compensate for their weaknesses (in encoding). Although they are rarely (purely) auditory learners, we must prepare them for learning through this modality.

Analyzing a student's preferred symbol set is the first step toward developing communication literacy. Most of us realize at an early age that letters and sounds have a relationship. This is important for reading and spelling, because ultimately, letters and sounds are blended to form spoken and written words. Many children on the spectrum will never make this connection, and at some point we must use alternative ways of improving their literacy.

Preferred symbol sets

In my experience, there are, by broad definition, five types of preferred symbol sets that autistic children tend to use: wholistic, phonetic, patterned logic, graphic, and topic focused. Unless you have a lot of extra time and energy on your hands, it is best to acknowledge this preference and to use this natural ability to strengthen the other forms of literacy.

WHOLISTIC SYMBOL SETS

Children who prefer this avenue are rarely tuned to details or components of words. They rarely respond to single sounds or a phonetic approach. Rather, they remember large chunks of words, sentences, even scripts to movies, commercials, or other phrases/sentences with repetitive components. They recognize insignias, marquee messages, symbols, brand names. They are known as "sight word" readers, users of "echolic speech," and they are rarely creative in expressing their own thoughts.

Phonics drills are usually frustrating to them because they do not relate letters and sounds to word structures. They skip immediately to larger components of communication. They are best taught using single message symbols and sight words. Introduce high interest words, functional-environmental symbols and "pivot words" that appear with great frequency in their spoken/written vocabulary. Rather than teach in isolation, begin with categories or large classifications, and work downward into smaller units of meaning. Use complementary strategies such as hands-on learning and thematic teaching to develop comprehension and generalization.

PHONETIC SYMBOL SETS

Children who have phonetic disorders have difficulty in relating sounds to graphic symbols. This ultimately affects their decoding ability and their spelling is compromised if teachers rely solely upon using a phonetic approach to teach these other two skill sets. Many children with autism have problems in understanding letter–sound relationships, and they must therefore receive special assistance in learning to understand them. Hyperlexia, on the other hand, is sometimes manifested in children with autism who are found to be "good readers" usually from an early age, and without having had any formal instruction. This accelerated ability in phonics, however, is deceptive to parents and teachers because, in contrast, they are generally poor in reading comprehension. Although these children are fascinated and very proficient about manipulating certain features of words (sounds, letters, unusual spellings, word similarities, etc.), this skill is often out of keeping with the other important aspects of reading. The meaningful application of words almost always lags behind this isolated skill in decoding and word recognition. They are prone to appear as mechanistic, inflexible readers, who are reliant upon certain, memorized rules from which they refuse to deviate. Children with hyperlexia and autism often have an "agenda" for what they want to read or spell; they rarely engage in recreational or social reading. They might win a presidential spelling bee, but they may never understand a passage beyond a third grade reading level. The goal for children with hyperlexia, therefore, is to expand their reading repertoire beyond this high interest focus. Their relative strength with hyperlexia should be used to facilitate learning in other academic or social areas. Remember, the caveat to their proficient spelling and decoding abilities is that they are seductive. Care should always be taken to assess for comprehension and to equalize this skill with reading recognition.

If you are skillful enough, you can help them to transfer this interest to new word elements or meaningful word usages (e.g., words with silent and double letters, words with more than one meaning, birth dates of family members, etc.). Do not be deceived into thinking that their advanced spelling or reading vocabularies equate to word understanding or comprehension. While these are children who make great proofreaders, they are relatively limited in their practical knowledge of the very same words they can spell. Emphasis should be on application, vocabulary expansion, syntax, and semantics rather than word decoding. Also use their strong memorization skills to help them learn new "rules" involving word organization, and spend time on both the less preferred and most preferred topic. If a student's organizational skills on a topic are well developed, transfer this strength through analogies, similarities, and other comparative means to the new, unfamiliar topic. Reading, spelling, vocabulary and any other assignments can involve both topics. Because these topics of fascination can lead to vocational choices, they should not be discouraged, but put into perspective.

PATTERNED LOGIC SYMBOL SETS

For children who have this orientation, literacy can be accomplished through repetition. The visual, spatial, and musical modalities are often helpful in facilitating this. Visual patterns (color and size gradations), musical patterns (melody, chant, beat, familiar tunes), or spatial patterns (hierarchies, top-down and left-to-right orientation, diagrams, and graphs) can offer emphasis to the spoken or written word, phrase, and sentence. By seeing patterns in groups of sounds, letters, words or other forms of communication, children can learn the logic of concepts such as prosody, syllabication, rhyme, negation, and noun–verb agreement.

GRAPHIC SYMBOL SETS

As we know there are a large number of students who fail to develop verbal speech. While this is an obstacle, it does not mean they will never advance in reading literacy. These students often have success in encoding and decoding communication through graphics: symbols, icons, pictures, keyboarding. There are several computer software programs that facilitate this type of communication. Teachers can develop literacy by creating individualized communication books that combine words with pictures and symbols to advance a child's understanding in a given area. Students who prefer graphics are very similar to those who are "wholistic" in their manner of communication. In general, these children will be less responsive to small units of meaning (e.g., sound–letter relationships, capital letters, etc.), and more responsive to high-interest or high-use ideas. They are also usually very visually oriented, so they will probably cue into the color, contrast, patterns, and size differences of graphics.

Students who are verbal may find graphic symbols helpful in literacy development, especially if they are used for structure and organization. Templates, webs, diagrams, and icons have already been discussed as assistive techniques for organizing a student's thoughts, both spoken and written, if a student struggles in keeping up with the volume expected in grammar, and structure of longer compositions (both oral and written).

TOPIC-FOCUSED SYMBOL SETS

Many children with autism are (relatively) proficient as either encoders or decoders, but they are focussed on a certain idea or topic. Their communication patterns tend to be perseverative and rigid. They have an incessant tendency to orient conversations back to their preference, making them appear idiosyncratic. The best way to deal with these types of children is to channel these preferences so that they only occur at a given time or place. If writing is a strength, allow them to journal their ideas. Build a bridge to another, somewhat related topic by having them focus on similarities and differences, or by providing experiences for keyboarding. If a student's handwriting is so labored that he cannot express his thoughts in written form, it is helpful to create an alternative way for him to demonstrate understanding of a particular concept in communication. For example, rather than insist that a student physically rewrite an essay to show understanding of sequence and reasoning, he could arrange pre-written sentences in correct order.

Developing higher forms of literacy

If we are lucky, we have at some time or other been under the spell of a great storyteller – that extraordinary person who can connect reality with the hypothetical; who can help us transcend our every-day experiences with a larger, more general, and meaningful content. I believe storytelling is helpful in advancing the literacy level of children with autism because it is a natural tool of communication used by many teachers, and many parents. It is a forum for a shared social experience, which in turn builds focus, joint attention, refer-encing, sequential memory, and symbolic communication.

Storytelling is an ancient custom that represents the highest form of communication – social meaning portrayal in stories. It connects reality with large-scale meaning through symbolism. It combines the powerful art form using the spoken word, sometimes with pictures, books, graphics, sometimes only with words, gestures, and mime. Storytelling is a natural communication device used in our culture to send social messages. It can develop the communicative literacy of students with autism in the following ways:

- telling social stories which relate to an upcoming event or changes, a highly significant happening, experiences of individual or groups of students

- sequencing a social exchange of real events and comparing them to a sequence of imagined or hypothetical events

- predicting outcomes of social dilemmas following an authentic, personal story

- interpreting surreal stories (cartoons, videos, movies, comic strips) for meaning

- identifying and inferring symbolic messages, events, actions given a high-interest situation

- using stories as reference points for understanding new experiences

- reinforcement/dovetailing of print reading

- students' role in storytelling should be expanded from a passive participation to active engagement whereby creativity and imagination is encouraged.

Developing the social graces

Helping children with autism acquire the social graces is the Olympian challenge of teachers because it is such a difficult, and relentless task. As the word grace implies, however, getting to social competency is arduous. It involves many seemingly invisible steps that culminate in the appearance of gracefulness. Unless we are the coaches, we cannot appreciate the hours of hard work, of personal challenge and despair, but we can see the final outcome. So it is with social gracefulness. It is a painstaking process for students and their coaches/teachers.

The theory of mind blindness explains their "social" problem better than any other I have encountered. Integrating and communicating information is a monumental hurdle for these children, but mastering both of these tasks within a social context is almost impossible without tedious analysis, practice, and corrections. It is easy to see why they are so comfortable with predictable routines and memorized information because these actions require little or no interpretation or judgement. Being "social" requires flexibility, quick decision making, deducing inferences and intent. Children with autism are sadly crippled in this area, and as teachers and therapists we must devote continuous and creative efforts to teach them the skills they need. Temple Grandin states:

> For people with autism, rules are very important, because we concentrate intensely on how things are done…many people have difficulty deciphering how people with autism understand rules. I don't have any social intuition, I rely on pure logic… I categorize rules according to their logical importance… It is a complex algorithmic decision-making drill. Emotion does not guide my decision; it is pure computing. (Grandin 1995, p.103)

Like any complex skill, social aptitude can be improved if it is taught in step-by-step fashion, in concrete terms, practiced, tested, and then generalized. Even the most basic social expectations do not come naturally because of shifts in context, meaning, and perception. Socialness is less explained by a "black and white" analogy, and more by a series of gradation of gray. In her recollection on growing up, Grandin laments:

> I had a strict moral upbringing, and I learned as a child that stealing, lying, and hurting people were wrong. As I grew older, I observed that it was all right to break certain rules, but not others. I constructed a program for rules…into three categories: "really bad," "sins of the system," and "illegal but not bad." (Grandin 1995, p.103)

We cannot always reach into their minds to know what they're thinking, but when one reads the wisdom of Temple Grandin and others with autism, we must be cognizant of their perceptions of our social rules. Using the interpersonal and intrapersonal intelligences is a highly sophisticated process that does not advance by "being around typical peers." Here are some ideas that have met with success in programs I have worked with: social inventories, social vocabularies, rehearsals, practice, scales for social concepts.

SOCIAL INVENTORIES

Survey the landscape of the environment that your child must function within. Observe teachers, students, support and administrative personnel (the cafeteria faculty and school bus attendants are as important to this child's success as the building principal). Prioritize social expectations and rules into two categories: major and minor. Then rank them by level of importance. In order to be realistic, focus on 10 to 12 of these, combined total. Examples of social skills might include:

- raising hand in request
- refraining from asking repetitive questions
- maintaining good hygiene
- refraining from dominating the play area.

Set a time frame for mastery – usually the high priority "major" rules take a long time. Conversely, you might be able to accomplish two lower priority, "minor" items in half the time. Allow a lot of time for developing these skills just as you would math or reading.

Social vocabularies

For each of the 10 to 12 social goals, select key vocabulary words that are necessary for mastery of each goal. When vocabulary words can be cross-referenced between goals, generalization and comprehension is increased. For example, if the concept "honesty" is critical to three social goals, the student will have more opportunities to learn it. Receptive, then expressive, practice of vocabulary should begin in isolated settings. Reinforce any spontaneous observance or use of these concepts that occur in natural settings.

Rehearsals

Choose older peers rather than same-age peers for rehearsals. Older students are more predictable and can usually carry out interactions which are more sophisticated than younger children. Rehearse in protected, isolated settings.

its to practice their social skills and social vocabularies cial contexts. If a student falters at this stage, pre-arrange events or familiar persons, but continue to practice in a natu...tting.

Scales for understanding and communicating abstract social concepts

Temple Grandin made an incredibly important point when she explained that she "thinks in pictures." From this we know that bringing visual elements into instructional situations helps to facilitate learning for many, if not most students with autism. Social skills instruction is no exception. Because of their strong sense of justice and the fact that they are "black and white" in their reasoning abilities, children with autism struggle in understanding the "gray" areas of the nuances and variations in how social skills are applied. Programs that teach specific, conditioned responses to use within social dialogues trap children with autism because they fail to build in the flexibility that they need when the social scenes change (which they invariably do).

I have found that by providing them with a visual scale of reasoning, they are more successful in grasping these ideas. For younger children, I typically recommend color or size gradations because this is usually within the scope of their development. For older children, or those with better developed cognitive skills, I use Likert scales or other concepts that they can personally relate to (mountain elevations, speed, movie characters or themes which are parallel). Figure 6.1 offers an example of how the concept of "being honest" could be visually represented, and depicts a basic, numerically scaled representation of the concepts of right and wrong. Figure 6.2 shows a scheme for politeness, using size gradation to represent importance of good choices (color would work as well).

Very wrong					No problem					Very right
-5	-4	-3	-2	-1	0	+1	+2	+3	+4	+5
Lying; cheating; misrepresenting; knowingly being dishonest		Distorting the facts in a way that will bring hardship to others hiding the truth						Telling the truth when requested by persons in a role of authority; seeking out those in authority to reveal the truth about a situation that will otherwise harm someone including self		Avoiding being critical of others to keep from hurting their feelings; choosing alternative words, actions, or refraining from commenting

Figure 6.1 Visual and numerical representation of "being honest" and the concepts of right and wrong

POLITE

RESPECTFUL

TO THE POINT

IMPOLITE

RUDE

Figure 6.2 Politeness scheme using size graduation

Digital photography and videotaping

These are two very worthwhile techniques that could have been placed in the section on visually cued instruction, but their effect is so powerful in teaching social-pragmatic language skills that they deserve a section of their own. Because of advancements in technology, there should be little reason not to take advantage of digital and video cameras and all of their computer-related features. Real time photography, as I call it, allows us to teach social relationships using pictures of people and situations which are most immediate and important to our students. Still and action photos and videos can demonstrate many key concepts: messages sent through facial expressions, body language and gestures, recognizing and displaying emotions, turn taking and using social amenities. We can teach more advanced techniques such as initiating and terminating conversations, "repairing" social mistakes, interpreting inferences, humor, and sarcasm. Videotapes are especially helpful in teaching students about social relationships and situations, and the communication patterns typically found in them. The most effective use of real time photography occurs when scripts, stories, and social stories are written in conjunction with them. Unlike our techniques for social skills training, photography paired with a written component is best used in small groups with other students rather than in isolation.

Scripts and stories developed for social experiences allow for individualized and therefore meaningful lesson components. Stories, books, and videos created as part of this social curriculum can be revisited as often as necessary. They can be checked out for home use so that parents can be a part of the process. They can be enjoyed as recreation during free time, and can be an integral part of a thematic teaching unit or a class project.

Real time photography can be useful at two critical junctures: before a social event occurs, and after the social experience. For students with autism, a prediction phase is very helpful prior to the actual event. Videos and pictures can be used to rehearse and practice key social behaviors. They can also be used to review an experience, to problem solve, and to identify new social concepts for future training. Everyone loves looking at themselves in pictures, and children with autism are no exception.

Social skills instruction is a thread that should run through a teacher's entire curriculum. It is true that many social-language concepts must be introduced in isolation, and practiced vigorously before they can be applied in meaningful ways. However, an effective teacher will have an obvious social skills "throughline" where there are opportunities planned at all levels, in individual, small, and large group settings. There should be an emphasis on social skills in each and every activity: math, reading, vocabulary, etc. Social success is a process, not an end point:

> My life was a series of incremental steps. I am often asked what the single breakthrough was that enabled me to adapt to autism. There was not a single breakthrough…it was a series of incremental improvements. (Grandin 1995, p.35)

Conclusion

It has been 25 years since Johnny and I shared a classroom. I have learned so much from the teachers and the parents who have allowed me to observe and share ideas about helping their children learn. They have inspired me, as Johnny did, to organize my ideas into the form of a book.

There is no quick fix for teaching children with autism. Despite all the advances in this field in the past three decades, I realize that this is as true today as it was when I worked with Johnny. It takes enduring perserverance, and endless energy. It requires that teachers blend theory and creativity, for every child is unique.

We have come a long way in recognizing and understanding autism since Kanner and Asperger wrote of their discoveries. Still, we cannot prevent autism, nor can we cure it. We can only hope to identify and treat it properly. To do so, we need the special expertise of the researchers and practitioners who have dedicated their talents and energy to this very special condition. We need teachers and therapists who can take these theories forward, who can analyze their day-to-day experiences, and who can creatively make changes in their instructional approach. Parents rely upon all of us to look to the future with realistic optimism, to offer direction and hope. As Temple Grandin says:

> There is no cure for autism, and parents must be cautious to avoid being misled by extravagant claims made by people who are promoting their own brand of therapy. Treatments that are

effective should work with a reasonable amount of effort. (Grandin 1995, p.222)

Every day, from this day forward, there will be a family who is told their child has autism. Elsewhere, a teacher will be informed that the new student in his or her class has autism. Parents and teachers, as partners, will be called upon to meet this challenge.

The past few decades of research, observation, and reflection have taught us that although autism is a lifelong condition, it is one that is changeable. As Dr. Grandin advises, given reasonable intervention and guidance, we can be optimistic about helping students with autism to make progress.

Teachers must orchestrate a learning environment that is developmentally appropriate, motivating, and functionally useful. This demands an intuitive blend of theory, creativity, and timing, for "teaching is an art, and the true teacher is an artist" (Dewey 1998b, p.288).

It is my hope that the ideas brought forth in this book will assist parents and teachers in this endeavor. In conclusion, I cannot stress strongly enough the importance of developing vital social relationships for all involved in this process: for students, for parents, and for educators.

References

Armstrong, T. (1987) *In Their Own Way: Discovering and Encouraging your Child's Personal Learning Style.* New York: Tarcher/Putnam-Penguin.

Armstrong, T. (1998) *Awakening Genius in the Classroom.* Alexandria, VA: ASCD.

Bandura, A. (1969) *Principles of Behavior Modification.* New York: Holt, Rinehart and Winston.

Bloom, B. and Krathwohl, D. (eds) (1976) *Taxonomy of Educational Objectives.* New York: Longman.

Bondy, A. and Frost, L. (1994) "The picture exchange communication system." *Focus on Autistic Behavior 9*, 3, 1–19.

Bondy, A. and Frost, L. (1998) "The picture exchange communication system." *Topics in Language Disorders 19*, 373–390.

Bruner, J. (1966) *Toward a Theory of Instruction.* Cambridge, MA: Harvard University Press.

Bruner, J. (1983) *Child's Talk: Learning to Use Language.* New York: Norton.

Caine, R. and Caine, G. (1997) *Education on the Edge of Possibility.* Alexandria, VA: ASCD.

Carroll, J. (1963) *A Model of School Learning.* New York: McGraw-Hill.

Denes, P. and Pinson, E. (1970) *The Speech Chain: The Physics and Biology of Spoken Language.* New York: Bell Telephone Laboratories. (First published 1963.)

Dewey, J. (1998a) *Experience and Education.* Boston, MA: Houghton Mifflin.

Dewey, J. (1998b) *How We Think.* Boston, MA: Houghton Mifflin.

Fennimore, T. and Tinzmann, M. (1990) *What is a Thinking Curriculum?* Oak Brook, IL: North Central Regional Educational Library.

Freeman, B. (1993) *The Advocate.* Washington, DC: Autism Society of America.

Frith, U. (2003) *Autism: Explaining the Enigma*, 2nd edn. Malden, MA: Blackwell.

Gardner, H. (1983) *Frames of Mind: The Theory of Multiple Intelligences.* New York: Basic Books.

Gardner, H. (1987a) "An individual-centered curriculum." In *The Schools We've Got, The Schools We Need.* Washington, DC: Council of Chief State School Officers and The American Association of Colleges of Teacher Education.

Gardner, H. (1987b) "Beyond IQ: Education and human development." *Harvard Educational Review 57*, 2, 187–193.

Gardner, H. (1991) *The Unschooled Mind: How Children Think, and How Schools Should Teach.* New York: Basic Books.

Gardner, H. (1993) *Creating Minds.* New York: Basic Books.

Gardner, H. (1997) "Multiple intelligences as a partner in school improvement." *Educational Leadership 55*, 1, 20–21.

Gardner, H. (1999) *Intelligence Reframed.* New York: Basic Books.

Grandin, T. (1995) *Thinking in Pictures.* New York: Vintage Books.

Gray, C. (1995) "Teaching children with autism to 'read' social situations." In K. Quill (ed) *Teaching Children with Autism: Strategies to Enhance Communication and Socialization.* New York: Delmar.

Greenspan, S. and Wieder, S. (1997) "An integrated developmental approach to interventions for young children with severe difficulties in relating and communicating." *Zero to Three 18*, 5–17.

Greenspan, S. and Wieder, S. (1998) *The Child with Special Needs: Encouraging Intellectual and Emotional Growth*. Reading, MA: Perseus Books.

Greenspan, S. and Wieder, S. (1999) "A functional developmental approach to autism spectrum disorders." *Journal of the Association for Severely Handicapped 24*, 3, 147–161.

Greenspan, S. and Wieder, S. (2000) "A developmental approach to difficulties in relating and communicating in autism spectrum disorders and related symptoms." In A. Wetherby and B. Prizant (eds) *Autism Spectrum Disorders: A Transactional Developmental Perspective*. Baltimore, MD: Paul H. Brookes.

Hamblin, R., Buckholdt, D., Ferritor, D., Kozloff, M., and Blackwell, L. (1971) *The Humanization Processes*. New York: Wiley.

Harris, S. and Weiss, M. (1998) *Right from the Start: Behavioral Interventions for Young Children with Autism*. Bethesda, MD: Woodbine House.

Hart, C. (1995) "Teaching children with autism: What parents want." In K. Quill (ed) *Teaching Children with Autism: Strategies to Enhance Communication and Socialization*. New York: Delmar.

Hermelin, B. and O'Connor, N. (1976) *Psychological Experiments with Autistic Children*. New York: Pergamon.

Hewett, F. (1965) "Teaching speech to an autistic child through operant conditioning." *American Journal of Orthopsychiatry 35*, 927–936.

Hodgdon, L. (1995) *Visual Strategies for Improving Communication*. Troy, MI: Quirk Roberts.

Hoerr, T. (2002) "Becoming an MI school." Presentation given at the Multiple Intelligences Institute, New City School, St. Louis, MO.

Hunter, M. (1976) *Rx: Improved Instruction*. El Segundo, CA: TIP Publications.

Hunter, M. (1979) "Diagnostic teaching." *Elementary School Journal 80*, 41–46.

Katz, L. and Chard, S. (1998) "Issues in selecting topics for projects." ERIC no. ED424031. Champaign, IL: ERIC Clearinghouse on Elementary and Early Childhood Education.

Kilpatrick, W. (1918) "The project method." *Teachers College Record 19*, 319–335.

Koegel, R. and Koegel, L. (eds) (1995) *Teaching Children with Autism: Strategies for Initiating Positive Interactions and Improving Learning Opportunities*. Baltimore, MD: Paul H. Brookes.

Koegel, R. and Koegel, L. (1996) *Positive Behavioral Support: Including People with Difficult Behavior in the Community*. Baltimore, MD: Paul H. Brookes.

Kovalik, S. (1993) *III: The Model: Integrated Thematic Instruction*, 2nd edn. Village of Oak Creek, AZ: Books for Educators.

Kovalik, S. and Olsen, K. (1997) *III: The Model: Integrated Thematic Instruction*, 3rd edn. Kent, WA: Books for Educators.

Kozloff, M. (1973) *Reaching the Autistic Child*. Champaign, IL: Research Press.

LaVigna, G. and Donnellan, A. (1986) *Alternatives to Punishment: Solving Behavior Problems with Non-Aversive Strategies*. New York: Irvington.

Lazear, D. (1991) *Seven Ways of Teaching: The Artistry of Teaching with Multiple Intelligences*. Palatine, IL: Skylight.

Lissner, K. (1992) "Insider's point of view." In E. Schopler and G. Mesibov (eds) *High Function Individuals with Autism*. New York: Plenum.

Lovaas, O. (1969) *Behavior Modification: Teaching Language to Psychotic Children* [Film]. New York: Appleton-Century-Croft.

Lovaas, O. (1977) *The Autistic Child: Language Development Through Behavior Modification*. New York: Irvington Press.

Lovaas, O. (2000) *Clarifying Comments on the UCLA Young Autism Project*. Los Angeles, CA: University of California, Department of Psychology.

Macaulay, R. (1994) *The Social Art: Language and its Uses*. New York: Oxford University Press.

McEachin, J., Smith, T., and Lovaas, O. (1993) "Long-term outcome for children with autism who received early intensive behavioral treatment." *American Journal of Mental Retardation 97*, 359–372.

McGee, G., Krantz, P., and McClannahan, L. (1986) "An extension of incidental teaching to reading instruction for autistic children." *Journal of Applied Behavior Analysis 19*, 147–157.

Maurice, C. (1993) *Let Me Hear Your Voice: A Family's Triumph Over Autism.* New York: Knopf.

Maurice, C., Green, G., and Fox, R. (eds) (2001) *Making a Difference: Behavioral Intervention for Autism.* Austin, TX: Pro-Ed Publishers.

Maurice, C., Green, G., and Luce, S. (eds) (1995) *Behavioral Interventions for Young Children with Autism.* Austin, TX: Pro-Ed Publishers.

Montessori, M. (1964) *The Montessori Method* (A.E. George, trans.) New York: Schocken Books.

Montessori, M. (1967) *The Absorbent Mind.* New York: Dell.

Montessori, M. (1972) *The Secret of Childhood.* New York: Ballantine.

National Research Council (2001) *Educating Children with Autism.* Committee on Educational Interventions for Children with Autism, Division of Behavioral and Social Sciences and Education. Washington, DC: National Academy Press.

Park, C. (1992) "Autism into art: A handicap transfigured." In E. Schopler and G. Mesibov (eds) *High Functioning Individuals with Autism.* New York: Plenum.

Pinker, S. (1997) *How the Mind Works.* New York: Norton.

Premack, D. (1959) "Toward empirical behavior laws: I. Positive reinforcement." *Psychological Review 66*, 219–233.

Premack, D. (1961) "Predicting instrumental performance from the independent rate of the contingent response." *Journal of Experimental Psychology 61*, 2, 163–171.

Premack, D. and Collier, G. (1962) *Analysis of Nonreinforcement Variables Affecting Response Probability.* Washington, DC: American Psychological Association.

Premack, D. and Premack, A. (2003) *Original Intelligence: Unlocking the Mystery of Who We Are.* New York: McGraw-Hill.

Prizant, B. and Wetherby, A. (1993) "Communication in preschool autistic children." In E. Schopler, M. van Bourgondieu, and M. Bristol (eds) *Preschool Issues in Autism.* New York: Plenum.

Prizant, B. and Wetherby, A. (1998) "Understanding the continuum of discrete trial traditional behavior to social-pragmatic developmental approaches in communication enhancement for young children with autism/PDD." *Seminars in Speech and Language 19*, 329–353.

Quill, K. (ed.) (1995) *Teaching Children with Autism: Methods to Enhance Communication and Socialization.* Albany, NY: Delmar.

Quill, K. (2000) *Do–Watch–Listen–Say: Social Communication Intervention for Children with Autism.* Baltimore, MD: Paul H. Brookes.

Skinner, B. (1974) *About Behaviorism.* New York: Vintage Books.

Styne, J. and Merrill, B. (1968) "People" (recorded by Barbra Streisand) On *Funny Girl*, produced by J. Gold, arranged and conducted by W. Scharf.

Sylwester, R. (1995) *A Celebration of Neurons: An Educator's Guide to the Human Brain.* Alexandria, VA: ASCD.

Treffert, D. (2000) *Extraordinary People: Understanding the Savant Syndrome.* New York: Harper and Row.

Vygotsky, L. (1962) *Thought and Language.* Cambridge, MA: MIT Press.

Wiggins, G. (1989) "A true test: Toward more authentic and equitable assessment." *Phi Delta Kappan 70*, 9 (May), 703–713.

Wiggins, G. (1993) *Assessing Student Performance: Exploring the Purpose and Limits of Testing.* San Francisco, CA: Jossey-Bass Publishers.

Further Reading

Adams, A. and Bebensee, E. (1983) *Success in Reading and Writing*. Glenview, IL: Goodyear.

Adams, M. (1992) *Beginning to Read: Thinking and Learning about Print*. Cambridge, MA: MIT Press.

Altbach, P., Kelly, P., Petrie, H., and Weis, L. (1991) *Textbooks in American Society*. Albany, NY: State University of New York Press.

Alvino, J. (1990) "A glossary of thinking skills terms." *Learning 18*, 6, 50.

American Music Therapy Association (2003) "How does music therapy make a difference for individuals with diagnoses on the autism spectrum?" www.musictherapy.org/factsheets/ autism.html (accessed July 20, 2003).

American Music Therapy Association (2003) "Why music therapy for individuals with diagnoses on the autism spectrum?" www.musictherapy.org/factsheets/autism.html (accessed July 20, 2003).

Anderson, J. (1983) *The Architecture of Cognition*. Cambridge, MA: Harvard University Press.

Anderson, M. (1992) *Intelligence and Development: A Cognitive Theory*. Oxford: Blackwell.

Anderson, M. (2001) "Annotation: Conceptions of intelligence." *Journal of Child Psychology and Psychiatry 42*, 287–298.

Anderson, S., Taras, M., and O'Malley, C. (1996) "Teaching new skills to young children with autism." In C. Maurice, G. Green, and S. Luce (eds) *Behavioral Interventions for Young Children with Autism*. Austin, TX: Pro-Ed.

Anzalone, M. and Williamson, G. (2001) "Sensory processing and motor performance in autism spectrum disorders." In A. Wetherby and B. Prizant (eds) *Children with Autism Spectrum Disorders: A Transactional Developmental Perspective*. Baltimore, MD: Paul H. Brookes.

Armbruster, B., Echols, C., and Brown, A. (1983) "The role of metacognition in reading to learn: A developmental perspective." Reading Education Report No. 40. Urbana, IL: Center for the Study of Reading.

Armbruster, R., Lehr, F., and Osborn, J. (2001) *Put Reading First. The Research Building Blocks for Teaching Children to Read: Kindergarten through Grade 3*. Washington, DC: Partnership for Reading.

Armstrong, T. (1984) "Learning differences – NOT learning disabilities." *Intelligence Connections*, fall.

Armstrong, T. (2000) *Multiple Intelligences in the Classroom*, 2nd edn. Alexandria, VA: ASCD.

Astington, J. (1993) *The Child's Discovery of the Mind*. Cambridge, MA: Harvard University Press.

Attwood, T. (1998) *Asperger's Syndrome: A Guide for Parents and Professionals*. London: Jessica Kingsley Publishers.

Axelrod, S. and Hall, R. (1999) *Behavior Modification: Basic Principles*, 2nd edn. Austin, TX: Pro-Ed.

Ayers, A. (1979) *Sensory Integration and the Child*. Los Angeles: Western Psychological Services.

Ayers, A. and Heskett, W. (1972) "Sensory integrative dysfunction in a young schizophrenic girl." *Journal of Autism and Childhood Schizophrenia 2*, 2, 174–181.

Ayers, A. and Tickle, L. (1980) "Hyper-responsivity to touch and vestibular stimuli as a predictor or positive response to sensory integration procedures by autistic children." *American Journal of Occupational Therapy 24*, 375–381.

Ayers, J. (1972) "Improving academic scores through sensory integration." *Journal of Learning Disabilities 5*, 338–343.

Baer, D. (1998) *How to Plan for Generalization*, 2nd edn. Austin, TX: Pro-Ed.

Bailey, R. and Gillespie, N. (2001) "Biology vs. The Blank Slate: Evolutionary Psychologist Steven Pinker Deconstructs the Great Myths about how the Mind Works." *Reason 34*, 5, 48–56.

Baker, B. and Brightman, A. (1997) *Steps to Independence: Teaching Everyday Skills to Children with Special Needs*, 3rd edn. Baltimore, MD: Paul H. Brookes.

Bandura, A. (1977) *Social Learning Theory*. Englewood Cliffs, NJ: Prentice-Hall.

Baratta-Lorton, M. (1972) *Workjobs: Activity-Centered Learning for Early Childhood Education*. Reading, MA: Addison-Wesley.

Baron-Cohen, S. (1990) "Autism: A specific cognitive disorder of mind-blindness." *International Review of Psychiatry 2*, 79–88.

Baron-Cohen, S. (1995) *Mindblindness: An Essay on Autism*. Cambridge, MA: MIT Press.

Baron-Cohen, S., Leslie, A., and Frith, U. (1985) "Does the autistic child have a 'theory of mind'?" *Cognition 21*, 37–46.

Barron, F. (1969) *Creative Person and Creative Process*. New York: Holt, Rinehart and Winston.

Bauer, C. (1993) *New Handbook for Storytellers*. Chicago: American Library Association.

Baum, R. (1990) "Finishing touches: Top 10 programs." *Learning 18*, 6, 51–55.

Beane, J. (1995) "Curriculum integration and the disciplines of knowledge." *Phi Delta Kappan 76*, 8, 616–622.

Begley, E. (1996) "How kids are wired for music, math, and emotions." *Newsweek*, February, 55–61.

Bellance, J., Chapman, C., and Swartz, E. (1994) *Multiple Assessments for Multiple Intelligences*. Palatine, IL: IRI/Skylight.

Bellenca, J. and Fogarty, R. (1990) *Blueprints for Cooperative Learning in the Thinking Classroom*. Palatine, IL: Skylight.

Bellenca, J. and Fogarty, R. (1993) *Catch Them Thinking – A Handbook of Classroom Strategies*. Palatine, IL: Skylight.

Berger, D. (2002) *Music Therapy, Sensory Integration and the Autistic Child*. London: Jessica Kingsley Publishers.

Berger, S. (1991) *Differentiating Curriculum for Gifted Students*. ERIC Clearinghouse on Disabilities and Gifted Education No. E510. Arlington, VA: ERIC Clearinghouse on Disabilities and Gifted Education.

Berger, S. (1991) *Developing Programs for Students of High Ability*. ERIC Clearinghouse on Disabilities and Gifted Education No. E502. Arlington, VA: ERIC Clearinghouse on Disabilities and Gifted Education.

Bettleheim, B. (1967) *The Empty Fortress*. New York: Free Press.

Beyer, B. (1985) "Critical thinking: What is it?" *Social Education 49*, 4, 270–276.

Blakely, E. and Spence, S. (1990) *Developing Metacognition*. ERIC Digest. Syracuse, NY: ERIC Clearinghouse on Information Resources.

Block, J. (1971) *Mastery Learning: Theory and Practice*. New York: Rinehart and Winston.

Block, J., Efthim, H., and Burns, R. (1989) *Building Effective Mastery Learning in Schools*. New York: Longman.

Bloom, B. (1976) *Human Characteristics and School Learning*. New York: McGraw-Hill.

Bloom, B. (1981) *All Our Children Learning*. New York: McGraw-Hill.

Bloom, B. (ed.) (1984) *Taxonomy of Educational Objectives*. New York: David McKay.

Bloom, L. (1970) *Language Development: Form and Function in Emerging Grammars*. Cambridge, MA: MIT Press.

Boggeman, S., Hoerr, T., and Wallach, C. (1996) *Succeeding with Multiple Intelligences: Teaching Through the Personal Intelligences.* St. Louis, MO: New City School.

Bonny, H. and Savary, L. (1990) *Music and Your Mind.* Barrytown, NY: Station Hill Press.

Booth, L., Donnelly, J., and Horton, J. (2000) *Serving Students with Autism: A Legal Perspective.* Wayne, PA: Oakstone Legal and Business Publishing.

Bouchard, T. (1994) "Genes, environment and personality." *Science 264*, 1700–1701.

Bransford, J., Brown, A., and Cocking, R. (eds) (1999) *How People Learn: Brain, Mind, Experience and School.* Washington, DC: Committee on Developments in the Science of Learning, National Research Council.

Brewer, C. and Campbell, D. (1991) *Rhythms of Learning: Creative Tools for Developing Lifelong Skills.* Tucson, AZ: Zephyr Press.

Brooks, J. and Brooks, M. (1993) *In Search of Understanding: The Case for Constructivist Classrooms.* Alexandria, VA: ASCD.

Brown, R. (1973) *A First Language: The Early Stages.* Cambridge, MA: Harvard University Press.

Brownell, M. (2002) "Musically adapted social stories to modify behaviors in students with autism: Four case studies." *Journal of Music Therapy 39*, 2, 117–144.

Bruner, J. (1986) *Actual Minds: Possible Worlds.* Cambridge, MA: Harvard University Press.

Bruner, J., Goodnow, J., and Austin, A. (1956) *A Study of Thinking.* New York: Wiley.

Brunt, J. (1996) "Caring thinking: The new intelligence." Paper presented to the Australian Association for the Education of the Gifted and Talented, Adelaide, South Australia.

Burns, M. (1975) *The I Hate Mathematics Book.* Boston: Little, Brown.

Burruss, J. and Kaenzig, L. (1999) "Introversion: The often forgotten factor impacting the gifted." *Virginia Association for the Gifted Newsletter 21*, 1, 1–4.

Caine, R. and Caine, G. (1991) *Making Connections: Teaching and the Human Being.* Alexandria, VA: ASCD.

Caine, R. and Caine, G. (1998) "Building a bridge between neurosciences and education: Cautions and possibilities." *NASSP Bulletin 82*, 598, 1–6.

Campbell, D. (2002) *The Mozart Effect: Tapping the Power of Music to Heal the Body, Strengthen the Mind, and Unlock the Creative Spirit.* New York: HarperCollins.

Campbell, L. and Campbell, B. (2000) *Multiple Intelligences and Student Achievement: Success Stories from 6 Schools.* Alexandria, VA: ASCD.

Campbell, L., Campbell, B., and Dickinson, D. (1996) *Teaching and Learning through Multiple Intelligences.* Needham Heights, MA: Allyn and Bacon.

Canfield, J. and Wells, H. (1976) *100 Ways to Enhance Self-Esteem in the Classroom.* Englewood Cliffs, NJ: Prentice-Hall.

Carr, E. and Durand, M. (1985) "Reducing behavior problems through functional communication training." *Journal of Applied Behavior Analysis 18*, 111–126.

Carr, E., Levin, L., McConnachie, G., Carlson, J., Kemp, D., and Smith, C. (1994) *Communication Based Interventions for Problem Behavior: A User's Guide for Producing Positive Change.* Baltimore, MD: Paul H. Brookes.

Carr, E. and Ogle, D. (1987) "K-W-L Plus: A strategy for comprehension and summarization." *Journal of Reading 30*, 7, 626–631.

Carr, E., Schreibman, L., and Lovaas, O. (1974) "Control of echolalic speech in psychotic children." *Journal of Abnormal Child Psychology 3*, 331–351.

Cash, A. (1999) "A profile of gifted individuals with autism: The twice-exceptional learner." *Roeper Review 22*, 22–27.

Chall, J. (1967) *Learning to Read: The Great Debate.* New York: McGraw-Hill.

Chall, J. and Conrad, S. (1991) *Should Textbooks Challenge Students? The Case for Easier or Harder Textbooks.* New York: Teachers College Press.

Chard, S. (1998) *The Project Approach: Making Curriculum Come Alive, Practical Guide #1.* New York: Scholastic.

Chard, S. (1998) *The Project Approach: Developing Curriculum with Children, Practical Guide #2.* New York: Scholastic.

Chomsky, N. (1968) *Language and Mind.* New York: Harcourt, Brace, Javanovich.

Chomsky, N. (1975) *Reflections on Language.* New York: Pantheon.

Chomsky, N. (1986) *Knowledge of Language: Its Nature, Origins, and Use.* Cambridge, MA: MIT Press.

Church, C., Alisanski, S., and Amanullah, S. (2002) "The social, behavioral, and academic experiences of children with Asperger's syndrome." *Focus on Autism and Other Developmental Disabilities 15*, 1, 12–20.

Clay, M. (1972) *Reading: The Patterning of Complex Behavior.* Auckland: Heinemann.

Clay, M. (1975) *What Did I Write? Beginning Writing Behavior.* Auckland: Heinemann.

Clay, M. (1979) *The Early Detection of Reading Difficulties,* 3rd edn. Portsmouth, NH: Heinemann.

Coalition of Essential Schools, Devans MA (2002) "The Common Principles." www.essentialschools.org/pub/ces_docs/about/phil/10cps (accessed July 10, 2003).

Cobb, V. (1972) *Science Experiments You Can Eat.* Philadelphia: Lippincott.

Collins, N. (1994) *Metacognition and Reading to Learn.* Bloomington, IN: ERIC Clearinghouse on Reading English and Communication.

Columbus Group (1991) Unpublished transcript of the meeting of the Columbus Group, Columbus, OH, July.

Combined Elementary Task Forces of the Metropolitan Omaha Educational Consortium (MOEC) (1999). "Principles of brain-based learning." University of Nebraska at Omaha. http://www.unocoe.unomaha.edu/brainbased.htm (accessed July 15, 2003).

Committee on Educational Interventions for Children with Autism, National Research Council (2001) *Educating Children with Autism.* Washington, DC: National Academy Press.

Commoner, B. (1974) *The Closing Circle: Nature, Man, and Technology.* New York: Bantam Books.

Cook, D. and Dunn, W. (1998) 'Sensory integration for students with autism.' In R. Simpson and B. Myles (eds) *Educating Children and Youth with Autism.* Austin, TX: Pro-Ed.

Costa, A. (ed) (1985) *Developing Minds: A Resource Book for Teaching Thinking.* Alexandria, VA: ASCD.

Costa, A. (ed) (1991) *Developing Minds: A Resource Book for Teaching Thinking and Programs for Teaching Thinking* (revised edn, vols 1 and 2). Alexandria, VA: ASCD.

Costa, A. and Lowery, L. (1989) *Techniques for Teaching Thinking.* Pacific Grove, CA: Midwest Publications.

Cotton, K. (1988) *Classroom Questioning: Close Up No. 5.* Portland, OR: Northwest Regional Educational Laboratory.

Csikzentmihalyi, M. (1990) *Flow: The Psychology of Optimal Experience.* New York: Harper and Row.

Cushman, K. (1989) "Asking the essential questions: curriculum development." *Old Horace 5,* 5.

Dabrowski, K. (1967) *Personality Shaping through Positive Disintegration.* Boston: Little, Brown.

Dabrowski, K. (1972) *Psychoneurosis is not an Illness.* London: Gruf.

Damasio, A. (1994) *Descarte's Error: Emotion, Reason, and the Human Brain.* New York: Grosset/Putnam.

D'Amico, J. (1977) "School-to-work systems: An overview of key issues and elements." In J. D'Amico, A. Phleps, and M. Anderson (eds) *School-to-Work Systems: An Overview of Key Issues, Elements, Policies, and Practices.* Oak Brook, IL: North Central Regional Educational Laboratory.

Dasser, V., and Ulbaek, I., and Premack, D. (1989) "The perception of intention." *Science 243*, 4889, 365–369.

Davis, D. (1994) *Telling Your Own Stories.* Little Rock, AR: August House.

Davis, O. and Hunkins, F. (1966) "Textbook questions: What thinking processes do they foster?" *Peabody Journal of Education 43*, 285–292.

Dawson, G. and Osterling, J. (1997) "Early intervention in autism." In M. Guralnick (ed.) *The Effectiveness of Early Intervention.* Baltimore, MD: Paul H. Brookes Publishing.

Dawson, G. and Watling, R. (2000) "Interventions to facilitate auditory, visual, and motor integration in autism: A review of the evidence." *Journal of Autism and Developmental Disorders 30*, 5, 415–421.

Deacon, T. (1997) *The Symbolic Species.* New York: Norton.

DeGangi, G. and Greenspan, S. (1989) *Test of Sensory Functions in Infants.* Los Angeles, CA: Western Psychological Services.

Dettmer, S., Simpson, R., Myles, B., and Ganz, J. (2000) "The use of visual supports to facilitate transition of students with autism." *Focus on Autism and Other Developmental Disabilities 15*, 3, 163–169.

Dewey, M. (1992) "Autistic eccentricity." In E. Schopler and G. Mesibov (eds) *High Functioning Individuals with Autism.* New York: Plenum Press.

Diechowski, M. (1991) "Emotional development and emotional giftedness." In N. Colengelo and G. Davis (eds) *Handbook of Gifted Education.* Boston: Allyn and Bacon.

Dirkes, M. (1985) "Metacognition: Students in charge of their thinking." *Roeper Review 8*, 2, 96–100.

Dodge, D. and Colker, L. (1988) *The Creative Curriculum*, 3rd edn. Washington, DC: Teaching Strategies.

Donnellan, A., LaVigna, G., Negri-Shoultz, N., and Fassbender, L. (1988) *Progress Without Punishment: Effective Approaches for Learners with Behavior Problems.* New York: Teachers College Press.

Donnelly, J. and Altman, R. (1994) "The autistic savant: Recognizing and serving the gifted student with autism." *Roeper Review 16*, 252–253.

Dreyfus, A. and Lieberman, R. (1981) "Perceptions, expectations, and interactions: The essential ingredients for a genuine classroom discussion." *Journal of Biological Education 15*, 2, 153–157.

Duke, N. and Pearson, P. (2002) "Effective practices for developing reading comprehension." In A.E. Farstrup and S.J. Samuels (eds) *What Research Has to Say about Reading Instruction*, 3rd edn. Newark, NJ: International Reading Association.

Dunlap, G. (1999) "Consensus, engagement, and family involvement for young children with autism." *Journal of the Association for Persons with Severe Handicaps 24*, 3, 222–225.

Dunlap, G. and Kern, L. (1993) "Assessment and intervention for children within the instructional curriculum." In J. Reichle and D. Wacker (eds) *Communicative Approaches to the Management of Challenging Behavior.* Baltimore, MD: Paul H. Brookes.

Dunlap, G., Kern-Dunlap, L., Clarke, S., and Robbins, F. (1991) "Functional assessment, curricular revision and severe behavior problems." *Journal of Applied Behavior Analysis 24*, 387–397.

Dunlap, G., Kern, L., dePerczel, M., Clarke, S., Wilson, D., Childs, K., White, R., and Falk, G. (1993) "Functional analysis of classroom variables for students with emotional and behavior challenges." *Behavior Disorders 18*, 275–291.

Dunlap, G., Kern, L., and Worcester, J. (2001) "ABA and academic instruction." *Focus on Autism and Other Developmental Disabilities 16*, 2, 129–136.

Dunn, R. and Dunn, K. (1978) *Teaching Students through their Individualized Learning Styles.* Reston, VA: Reston.

Dunn, W. (1991) "The sensorimotor systems: A framework for assessment and intervention." In F. Orelove and D. Sobsey (eds) *Educating Children with Multiple Disabilities: A Transdisciplinary Approach*, 2nd edn. Baltimore, MD: Paul H. Brookes.

Dunn, W. (1997) "The impact of sensory processing abilities on the daily lives of young children and their families: A conceptual model." *Infants and Young Children 9*, 23–35.

Dunn, W. (2001) "The sensations of everyday life: Empirical, theoretical, and pragmatic considerations." *American Journal of Occupational Therapy 55*, 608–620.

Dunn, W., Saiter, J., and Rinner, L. (2002) "Asperger syndrome and sensory processing: A conceptual model and guidance for intervention planning." *Focus on Autism and Other Developmental Disabilities 17*, 3, 172–185.

Dunn, W. and Westman, K. (1997) "The sensory profile: The performance of a national sample of children without disabilities." *American Journal of Occupational Therapy 51*, 25–34.

Edelsky, C., Altwerger, B., and Flores, B. (1991) *Whole Language: What's the Difference?* Portsmouth, NH: Heinemann.

Edwards, D. and Mercer, N. (1987) *Common Knowledge: The Development of Understanding in the Classroom.* London: Methuen.

Egan, K. (1986) *Teaching as Story Telling: An Alternative Approach to Teaching and Curriculum in the Elementary School.* Ontario: University of Chicago Press.

Egan, K. (2003) "Start with what the student knows or with what the student can imagine?" *Phi Delta Kappan 84*, 6, 443–445.

Eisenberger, L. (1995) "The social construction of the human brain." *American Journal of Psychiatry 152*, 1563–1575.

Esveldt-Dawson, K. and Kazdin, A. (1998) *How to Maintain Behavior*, 2nd edn. Austin, TX: Pro-Ed.

Etzioni, A. (1996) *The New Golden Rule.* New York: Basic Books.

Evans, J. (ed.) (1983) *Thinking and Reasoning.* London: Routledge and Kegan Paul.

Evans, J., Wilson, B., Schuri, U., Andrade, J., Baddeley, A., Bruna, O., Canavan, T. *et al.* (2000) "A comparison of 'errorless' and 'trial and error' learning methods for teaching individuals with acquired memory disorders." *Neuropschological Rehabilitation 10*, 1, 67–110.

Feldman, D. and Goldsmith, L. (1986) *Nature's Gambit: Child Prodigies and the Development of Human Potential.* New York: Basic Books.

Flavell, J. (1988) "The development of children's knowledge about the mind: From cognitive connections to mental representations." In J. Astington, P. Harris, and D. Olson (eds) *Developing Theories of Mind.* New York: Cambridge University Press.

Flavell, J. (1999) "Cognitive development: Children's knowledge about the mind." *Annual Review of Psychology 50*, 21–45.

Flavell, J. and McGimsey, J. (1993) "Creating an optimal learning environment." In R. Houten and S. Axelrod (eds) *Behavior Analysis and Treatment.* New York: Plenum Publishers.

Fogarty, R. (1991) *The Mindful School: How to Integrate the Curricula.* Palatine, IL: DRI/Skylight.

Fogarty, R. and Stoehr, J. (1991) *Integrating Curricula with Multiple Intelligences: Teams, Themes, and Threads.* Palatine, IL: Skylight.

Fogelin, R. and Sinnott-Armstrong, W. (1991) *Understanding Arguments: An Introduction to Informal Logic.* Boston: Harcourt, Brace, Janovich.

Folstein, S. and Rutter, M. (1977) "Infantile autism: A genetic study of 21 twin pairs." *Journal of Child Psychology and Psychiatry 18*, 297–321.

Forest, H. (2000) "Listening, observing, remembering, practicing an ancient way of learning." www.storyarts.org/articles/listening.html (accessed July 19, 2003).

French, J. and Rhoder, C. (1992) *Teaching Thinking Skills: Theory and Practice.* New York: Garland.

Frith, U. (1978) "From print to meaning and from print to sound, or how to read without learning to spell." *Visible Language 12*, 43–54.

Frith, U. (1989) *Autism: Explaining the Enigma.* Oxford: Blackwell.

Frith, U. (ed.) (1991) *Autism and Asperger Syndrome.* New York: Cambridge University Press.

Frith, U. (1993) "Autism." *Scientific American 286*, 108–114.

Frith, U. (1995) "Autism: Beyond 'theory of the mind.'" *Cognition 50*, 13–30.

Frith, U. and Frith, C. (1999) "Interacting minds: A biological basis." *Science 286*, 1692–1695.

Frith, U., Happé, F., and Siddons, F. (1994) "Autism and theory of mind in everyday life." *Social Development 3*, 2, 108–124.

Gabbert, B., Johnson, D., and Johnson, R. (1986) "Cooperative learning, group-to-individual transfer, process gain, and the acquisition of cognitive reasoning strategies." *Journal of Psychology 120*, 265–278.

Gagne, R. (1977) *The Conditions of Learning*, 3rd edn. New York: Holt, Reinhart and Winston.

Gall, M. (1970) "The use of questions in teaching." *Review of Educational Research 40*, 5, 207–220.

Gall, M. (1984) "Synthesis of research on teacher questioning." *Educational Leadership 42*, 3, 40–46.

Gardner, H. (1990) "Building on the range of human strength." *The Churchill Forum 12*, 1, 1, 2, 7.

Gardner, H. (1995) "Reflections on multiple intelligences: Myths and messages." *Phi Delta Kappan 78*, 3, 200–203, 206–209.

Gardner, H. (1997) *Extraordinary Minds.* New York: Basic Books.

Gardner, H. and Hatch, T. (1989) "Multiple intelligences go to school." *Educational Researcher 18*, 8.

Genaux, M. and Maloney, M. (1999) *Building a Blueprint for Defensible Autism Programs.* Alexandria, VA: LRP.

Gentile, J. (1988) *Instructional Improvement: Summary and Analysis of Madeline Hunter's Essential Elements of Instruction and Supervision.* Oxford, OH: National Staff Development Council.

Ghaziuddin, M., Butler, E., Tsai, L., and Ghaziuddin, N. (1994) "Is clumsiness a marker for Asperger syndrome?" *Journal of Intellectual Disability Research 38*, 519–527.

Gibbs, J. (1987) *Tribes: A Process for Social Development and Cooperative Learning.* Santa Rosa, CA: Center Source.

Gillberg, C. (1989) *Diagnosis and Treatment of Autism.* New York: Plenum Press.

Gillberg, C. (2002) *A Guide to Asperger's Syndrome.* New York: Cambridge University Press.

Gillberg, C. and Coleman, M. (2000) *The Biology of the Autistic Syndromes*, 3rd edn. London: MacKeith Press and Cambridge University Press.

Glaser, R. (1984) "Education and thinking: The role of knowledge." *American Psychologist 39*, 93–104.

Goleman, D. (1995) *Emotional Intelligence.* New York: Bantam Books.

Goodlad, J. (1984) *A Place Called School.* New York: McGraw-Hill.

Gough, D. (1991) *Thinking About Thinking.* Alexandria, VA: National Association of Elementary School Principals.

Gould, S. (1980) *The Panda's Thumb.* New York: Norton.

Gould, S. (1994) "Curveball." *The New Yorker*, 28 November, 139–149.

Gould, S. (1996) *The Mismeasure of Man.* Harmondsworth: Penguin.

Grandin, T. (1995) "How people with autism think." In E. Schopler and G. Mesibov (eds) *Learning and Cognition in Autism.* New York: Plenum Publishers.

Gray, C. (1994) "Social interventions with high-functioning people with autism." Paper presented at the conference of the Treatment and Education of Autistic Children and Other Communication Handicapped Children (TEACCH), Chapel Hill, NC, May.

Gray, C. and Barand, J. (1993) "Social Stories: Improving responses of students with autism with accurate social information." *Focus on Autistic Behavior 8*, 1–10.

Green, G. (2001) "Behavior analytic instruction for learners with autism: Advances in stimulus control technology." *Focus on Autism and Other Developmental Disabilities 16*, 2, 72–85.

Greenspan, S. (1989) *The Essential Partnership*. New York: Viking Penguin.

Grubb, W. (1996) "The new vocationalism: What it is, What it could be." *Phi Delta Kappan 77*, 8, 535–540.

Grzywacz, P. and Lombardo, L. (1999) *Serving Students with Autism: The Debate Over Effective Therapies*. Horsham, PA: LRP.

Guilford, J. (1950) "Creativity." *American Psychologist 5*, 444–454.

Guilford, J. (1967) *The Nature of Human Intelligence*. New York: McGraw-Hill.

Guilford, J. (1977) *Way Beyond the IQ: Guide to Improving Intelligence and Creativity*. Buffalo, NY: Creative Education Foundation.

Guilford, J. and Hoepfner, R. (1971) *The Analysis of Intelligence*. New York: McGraw-Hill.

Guskey, T. (1997) *Implementing Mastery Learning*, 2nd edn. Stamford, CT: Wadsworth.

Gutstein, S. and Whitney, T. (2002) "Asperger syndrome and the development of social competence." *Focus on Autism and Other Developmental Disabilities 17*, 3, 161–171.

Habermas, J. (1971) *Knowledge and Human Interests* (J. Shapiro, trans.). Boston, MA: Beacon Press.

Hall, R. and Hall, M. (1998) *How to Select Reinforcers*, 2nd edn. Austin, TX: Pro-Ed.

Hanna, S. (1990) *A Professional Development Program Guide: Floortime – Tuning into Each Child*. New York: Scholastic.

Happe, F. (1995) *Autism: An Introduction to Psychological Theory*. Cambridge, MA: Harvard University Press.

Harmin, M. (1994) *Inspiring Active Learning: A Handbook for Teachers*. Alexandria, VA: ASCD.

Hart, B. (1985) "Naturalistic language training techniques." In S. Warren and A. Rogers-Warren (eds) *Teaching Functional Language: Generalization and Maintenance of Language Skills*. Baltimore, MD: University Park Press.

Hart, C. (1989) *Without Reason*. New York: Harper and Row.

Hart, L. (1975) *How the Brain Works*. New York: Basic Books.

Hart, L. (1981) "Don't teach them; help them learn." *Learning 9*, 8, 39–40.

Hart, L. (1983) *Human Brain and Human Learning*. Washington, DC: Books for Educators.

Heflin, L. and Simpson, R. (1998) "Interventions for children and youth with autism." *Focus on Autism and Other Developmental Disabilities 13*, 4, 194–211.

Heiman, M. and Slomianko, J. (eds) (1987) *Thinking Skills Instruction: Concepts and Techniques*. Washington, DC: National Education Association.

Hein, G. (1991) "Constructivist learning theory." Paper presented at the International Committee of Museum Educators conference, Jerusalem, Israel, 15–22 October.

Herman, J., Aschbacher, P., and Winters, L. (1992) *A Practical Guide to Alternative Assessment*. Alexandria, VA: ASCD.

Hermelin, B., O'Connor, N., and Lee, S. (1987) "Musical inventiveness of five idiot savants." *Psychological Medicine 17*, 685–694.

Herrnstein, R. and Murray, C. (1994) *The Bell Curve*. New York: Free Press.

Hoehn, L. and Birely, M. (1988) "Mental process preferences of gifted children." *Illinois Council for the Gifted Journal 7*, 28–31.

Hoerr, T. (1998) "Using multiple intelligences for students and faculty success." In R. Bernhardt, C. Hedley, G. Cattaro, and S. Vasilios (eds) *Curriculum Leadership: Rethinking Schools for the 21st Century*. Cresskill, NJ: Hampton Press.

Hoerr, T. (1999) "Redefining literacy: Other ways to learn." *Iowa Educational Leadership 2*, 2, 1, 4–5.

Hoerr, T. (2000) *Becoming a Multiple Intelligences School*. Alexandria, VA: ASCD.

Hoerr, T. (2001) "Excellence vs. perfection: Maintaining the balance." *ASCD: Classroom Leadership Online 4*, 5.

Hoerr, T. (2002) "Applying MI in Schools." Seattle, WA: New Horizons for Learning. www.newhorizons.org/strategies/mi/hoerr2.htm (accessed July 19, 2003).

Hollingworth, L. (1926) *Gifted Children: Their Nature and Nurture*. New York: Macmillan.

Hollingworth Center for Highly Gifted Children (2003) "Who are the highly gifted?" www.hollingworth.org/highlygifted.html (accessed July 13, 2003).

Hunter, M. and Carlson, P. (1971) *Improving Your Child's Behavior*. Glendale, CA: Bowmar.

Inhelder, B. and Piaget, J. (1969) *The Early Growth of Logic in the Child*. New York: Norton.

Itard, J. (1862) *The Wild Boy of Averon* (G. Humphrey and M. Humphrey, trans.) New York: Appleton-Century-Crofts. (Original work published 1807.)

Jacobs, H. (ed) (1989) *Interdisciplinary Curriculum: Design and Implementation*. Alexandria, VA: ASCD.

Jacobs, H. (1991) "The integrated curriculum?" *Instructor 101*, 2, 22–23.

Jewell, P. (1996) "A reasoning taxonomy for gifted education?" Paper presented to the Australian Association for the Education of the Gifted and Talented, Adelaide, South Australia.

Joyce, B. and Showers, B. (1983) *Power in Staff Development Through Research in Training*. Alexandria, VA: Association for Supervision and Curriculum Development.

Joyce, B. and Showers, B. (1995) *Student Achievement through Staff Development*, 2nd edn. New York: Longman.

Kain, D. (1993) "Cabbages – and kings: Research direction in integrated/interdisciplinary curriculum." *Journal of Educational Thought 27*, 3, 312–331.

Kanner, L. (1943) "Autistic disturbances of affective contact." *Nervous Child 2*, 217–250.

Kanner, L. (1946) "Irrelevant and metaphorical language in early infantile autism." *American Journal of Psychiatry 103*, 242–246.

Karweit, D. (1993) *Contextual Learning: A Review and Synthesis*. Baltimore, MD: Center for the Social Organization of Schools, Johns Hopkins University.

Kearney, K.L. (1992) "Life in the asynchronous family." *Understanding Our Gifted 4*, 6, 8–12.

Kearney, K.L. (1996) "Highly gifted children in full inclusion classrooms." *Highly Gifted Children 12*, 4.

Keefe, J. and Walberg, H. (eds) (1992) *Teaching for Thinking*. Reston, VA: National Association of Secondary School Principles.

Kelley, D. (1988) *The Art of Reasoning*. London: Norton.

King, L. (1987) "A sensory-integrative approach to the education of the autistic child." *Occupational Therapy in Health Care 24*, 2, 77–85.

Klin, A., Schultz, R., and Cohen, D. (2000) "Theory of mind in action: Developmental perspectives on social neuroscience." In S. Baron-Cohen, H. Tager-Flusberg, and D. Cohen (eds) *Understanding Other Minds: Perspectives in Developmental Neuroscience*. Oxford: Oxford University Press.

Klin, A. and Volkmar, F. (2000) "Treatment and intervention guideline for individuals with Asperger syndrome." In A. Klin, F. Volkmar, and S. Sparrow (eds) *Asperger Syndrome*. New York: Guilford Press, pp.340–366.

Klin, A., Volkmar, F.R., and Sparrow, S. (1992) "Autistic social dysfunction: Some limitations of the theory of mind hypothesis." *Journal of Child Psychology and Psychiatry 33*, 5, 861–876.

Klin, A., Volkmar, F.R., and Sparrow, S. (eds) (2000) *Asperger Syndrome*. New York: Guilford Press.

Knoll, M. (1997) "The project method: Its vocational education, origin and international development." *Journal of Industrial Teacher Education 34*, 3, 59–80.

Koegel, R., Camarata, S., Koegel, L., Ben-Tall, A., and Smith, A. (1998) "Increasing speech intelligibility in children with autism." *Journal of Autism and Developmental Disorders 28*, 3, 241–251.

Koegel, R., O'Dell, M., and Dunlap, G. (1998) "Producing speech use in nonverbal autistic children by reinforcing attempts." *Journal of Autism and Developmental Disorders 18*, 525–538.

Kohler, F., Strain, P., Hoyson, M., and Jamieson, B. (1997) "Combining incidental teaching and peer-mediation with young children with autism." *Focus on Autism and Other Developmental Disorders 12*, 196–206.

Kornhaber, M. and Gardner, H. (1991) "Critical thinking across multiple intelligences." In S. Maclure and P. Davies (eds) *Learning to Think: Thinking to Learn: The Proceedings of the 1989 DECD Conference.* Oxford: Pergamon Press, pp.147–168.

Koul, R., Scholosser, R., and Sancibrian, S. (2001) "Effects of symbol, referent, and instructional variables on the acquisition of aided and unaided symbols by individuals with autism spectrum disorders." *Focus on Autism and Other Developmental Disabilities 16*, 3, 162–169.

Kozloff, M. (1974) *Educating Children with Learning and Behavior Problems.* New York: Wiley.

Krantz, P. and McClannahan, L. (1993) "Teaching children with autism to initiate to peers: Effects of a script-fading procedure." *Journal of Applied Behavior Analysis 26*, 121–132.

Krantz, P. and McClannahan, L. (1998) "Social interaction skills for children with autism: A script-fading procedure for beginning readers." *Journal of Applied Behavior Analysis 31*, 191–202.

Krantz, P., MacDuff, M., and McClannahan, L. (1993) "Programming participation in family activities for children with autism: Parents' use of photographic activity schedules." *Journal of Applied Behavior Analysis 26*, 137–138.

Krathwohl, D., Bloom, B., and Masia, B. (1964) *Taxonomy of Educational Objectives: Handbook II: The Affective Domain.* New York: David McKay.

Lackney, J. (1998) "12 design principles based on brain-based learning research." Presentation at the CEFPI Midwest Regional Conference. www.designshare.com/research/ bainbasedlearn98.htm (accessed July 13, 2002).

Lake, K. (1994) "Integrated curriculum." Portland, OR: Northwest Regional Educational Laboratory. www.nwrel.org/scpd/sios (accessed July 30, 2003).

Landa, R. (2000) "Special language use in Asperger Syndrome and high functioning autism." In A. Klin, F.R. Volkmar, and S. Sparrow (eds) *Asperger Syndrome.* New York: Guilford Press, pp.125–155.

Langrehr, J. (1995) "Why do we need gifted programs?" *Australian Journal of Gifted Education 13*, 1.

Layton, T. and Watson, L. (1995) "Enhancing communication in non-verbal children with autism." In K. Quill (ed.) *Teaching Children with Autism: Strategies to Enhance Communication and Socialization.* New York: Delmar Publishers, pp.73–103.

Lazear, D. (2000) *The Intelligent Curriculum: Using Multiple Intelligences to Develop Your Students' Full Potential.* Tucson, AZ: Zephyr Press.

Levande, D. (1999) "Gifted readers and reading instruction." *CAG Communicator 30*, 19–20, 41–42.

Levine, D. (1985) *Improving Student Achievement Through Mastery Learning Programs.* San Francisco, CA: Jossey-Bass.

Lindsley, O. (1965) "Can deficiency produce specific superiority: The challenge of the idiot savant." *Exceptional Children 31*, 225–232.

Lindsley, O. (1971) "Precision teaching in perspective: An interview with Ogden R. Lindsley." *Teaching Exceptional Children 3*, 3, 114–119.

Lipman, M. (1994) "Caring thinking?" Paper presented at the Sixth International Conference on Thinking, Massachusetts Institute of Technology, Boston, July.

Lipson, M., Valencia, S., Wixson, K., and Peters, C. (1993) "Integration and thematic teaching: Integration to improve teaching and learning." *Language Arts 70,* 4, 252–264.

Little, C. (2001) "A closer look at gifted children with disabilities." *Gifted Child Today Magazine 24,* 3, 46–64.

Little, C. (2002) "Which is it? Asperger's syndrome or giftedness? Defining the difference." *Gifted Child Today Magazine 25,* 1, 58–63.

Longstreet, W. and Shane, H. (1993) *Curriculum for a New Millennium.* Boston, MA: Allyn and Bacon.

Lord, C. (1993) "Early social development in autism." In E. Schopler, M. Van Bourgondien, and M. Bristol (eds) *Preschool Issues in Autism.* New York: Plenum Publishers.

Lord, C. and Pickles, A. (1996) "Language level and nonverbal social communicative behaviors in autistic and language delayed children." *Journal of the American Academy of Child and Adolescent Psychiatry 35,* 11, 1542–1550.

Lord, C. and Risi, S. (2000) "Diagnosis of autism spectrum disorders in young children." In A. Wetherby and B. Prizant (eds) *Autism Spectrum Disorders: A Transactional Developmental Perspective.* Baltimore, MD: Paul H. Brookes.

Lovaas, O., Ackerman, A., Alexander, D., Firestone, P., Perkins, J., and Young, D. (1981) *Teaching Developmentally Disabled Children: The ME Book.* Austin, TX: Pro-Ed.

Luria, A. (1987) *The Mind of a Mnemonist.* Cambridge, MA: Harvard University Press.

McClannahan, L. and Krantz, P. (1999) *Activity Schedules for Children with Autism: Teaching Independent Behavior.* Bethesda, MD: Woodbine House.

McGee, G., Daly, T., Izeman, S., Man, L., and Risley, T. (1991) "Use of classroom materials to promote preschool engagement." *Teaching Exceptional Children 23,* 44–47.

McGee, G., Morrier, M., and Daly, T. (1999) "An incidental teaching approach to early intervention for toddlers with autism." *Journal of the Association for Persons With Severe Handicaps 24,* 133–146.

McGinnis, E. and Goldstein, A. (1984) *Skillstreaming the Elementary School Child: A Guide for Teaching Prosocial Skills.* Champaign, IL: Research Press.

McGinnis, E. and Goldstein, A. (1991) *Skillstreaming in Early Childhood.* Champaign, IL: Research Press.

McKim, R. (1980) *Experiences in Visual Thinking.* Monterey, CA: Brooks-Cole.

MacLeish, R. (1984) "Gifted by nature, prodigies are still mysteries to man." *Smithsonian Magazine,* March, 71–79.

Maguire, J. (1985) *Creative Storytelling: Choosing, Inventing, and Sharing Tales for Children.* Cambridge, MA: Yellow Moon Press.

Maker, C. (1986) *Critical Issues in Gifted Education,* Vol. 1. Austin, TX: Pro-Ed.

Marcus, L., Schopler, E., and Lord, C. (2000) "TEACCH services for preschool children." In J.S. Handleman and S. Harris (eds) *Preschool Education Programs for Children with Autism.* Austin, TX: Pro-Ed.

Margulies, N. (1991) *Mapping Inner Space: Learning and Teaching Mind Mapping.* Tucson, AZ: Zephyr Press.

Martin, J. (1995) "A philosophy of education for the year 2000." *Phi Delta Kappan 76,* 5, 355–359.

Marzano, R., Brandt, R., Hughes, C., Jones, B., Presseisen, B., Rankin, S., and Suhor, C. (1988) *Dimensions of Thinking: A Framework for Curriculum and Instruction.* Alexandria, VA: ASCD.

Meeker, M. (1969) *The Structure of the Intellect: Its Interpretations and Uses.* Columbus, OH: Merrill.

Merritt, S. (1990) *Mind, Music, and Imagery: 40 Exercises Using Music to Stimulate Creativity and Self Awareness.* New York: NAL/Plume.

Merton, T. (1979) *Love and Living.* New York: Farrar, Straus and Groux.

Mid-Continent Regional Educational Laboratory (1985) *Report of Thinking Skill Instructional Activities*. Denver, CO: Mid-Continent Regional Educational Laboratory.

Miller, J., Cassie, B., and Drake, S. (1991) *Holistic Learning: A Teacher's Guide to Integrated Studies*. Toronto: OISE Press.

Miller, L. (1988) *Miller Assessment for Preschools*. San Antonio, TX: Psychological Corporation.

Minogue, B. (1923) "A case of secondary mental deficiency with musical talent." *Journal of Applied Psychology 7*, 349–357.

Morelock, M. (1992) "Giftedness: The view from within." *Understanding Our Gifted 4*, 3, 11–15.

Morelock, M. and Feldman, D. (1993) "Prodigies and savants: What they tell us about giftedness and talent." In K. Heller, F. Monks, and A. Passow (eds) *International Handbook for Research on Giftedness and Talented*. Oxford: Pergamon Press, pp.161–181.

Mundy, P., Sigman, M., and Kasari, C. (1990) "A longitudinal study of joint attention and language development in autistic children." *Journal of Autism and Developmental Disorders 20*, 115–128.

Mundy, P., Sigman, M., Ungerer, J., and Sherman, T. (1987) "Nonverbal communication and play correlates of language development in autistic children." *Journal of Autism and Developmental Disorders 17*, 3, 349–364.

National Center for Clinical Infant Programs (1992) "Heart start: The emotional foundations of school success." In D. Goleman *Emotional Intelligence*. New York: Bantam.

NDT Resource Center (2003) "Practicing Effective Questioning." www.ndt.ed.org/teachingresources/classroomtips/effectivequestioning (accessed June 30, 2003).

Neilhart, M. (2000) "Gifted children with Asperger's syndrome." *Gifted Child Quarterly 44*, 222–230.

O'Connell, T. (1974) "The musical life of an autistic boy." *Journal of Autism and Childhood Schizophrenia 4*, 3, 223–229.

Ogle, D. (1986) "K–W–L: A teaching model that develops active reading of expository text." *The Reading Teacher 39*, 564–576.

Ogletree, B. and Oren, T. (1998) "Structured yet functional: An alternative conceptualization of treatment for communication impairment in autism." *Focus on Autism and Other Developmental Disabilities 13*, 4, 228–233.

On Purpose Associates (1998–2001) "Brain-based learning." www.funderstanding.com/brain_based_learning.cfm (accessed July 13, 2003).

O'Neill, R., Horner, R., Albin, R., Stoney, K., and Sprague, J. (1990) *Functional Analysis of Problem Behavior: A Practical Assessment Guide*. Sycamore, IL: Sycamore Publishing.

Oren, T. and Ogletree, B. (2000) "Program evaluation in classrooms for students with autism: Student outcomes and program processes." *Focus on Autism and Other Developmental Disabilities 15*, 2, 170–175.

Ornitz, E. (1970) "Vestibular dysfunction in schizophrenia and childhood autism." *Comprehensive Psychiatry 11*, 159–173.

Ornitz, E. (1974) "The modulation of sensory input and motor output in autistic children." *Journal of Autism and Childhood Schizophrenia 4*, 3, 197–215.

Osborne, L. (2000) "The little professor syndrome." *New York Times Magazine*, 18 June.

Ostrander, S. and Schroeder, L. (1979) *Superlearning*. New York: Delta.

Overly, N. (ed.) (1979) *Life-long Learning: A Human Agenda*. Alexandria, VA: Association for Supervision and Curriculum Development.

Ozonff, S. and Miller, J. (1995) "Teaching theory of mind: A new approach to social skills training for individuals with autism." *Journal of Autism Developmental Disorders 25*, 415–433.

Palincsar, A. (1986) "Metacognitive strategy instruction." *Exceptional Children 53*, 2, 118–124.

Palmer, P. (1993) *To Know as We Are Known: Education as a Spiritual Journey*. New York: HarperCollins.

Panyam, M. (1998) *How to Teach Social Skills*. Austin, TX: Pro-Ed.

Paris, K. (1994) *A Leadership Model for Planning and Implementing Change for School-to-Work Transition*. Madison, WI: Center on Education and Work, University of Wisconsin.

Park, D. and Youderian, P. (1974) "Light and number: Ordering principles in the world of an autistic child." *Journal of Autism and Childhood Schizophrenia 4*, 313–323.

Parker, J. (1989) *Instructional Strategies for Teaching the Gifted*. Boston, MA: Allyn and Bacon.

Passow, A. (1982) "Differentiating curricula for the gifted/talented." In *Selected Proceedings for the First National Conference in Curricula for the Gifted/Talented*. Ventura, CA: National/State Leadership Training Institute on the Gifted and Talented, pp.4–20.

Paul, R. (1985) "Critical thinking research: A response to Stephen Norris." *Educational Leadership 42*, 8, 46.

Paul, R. (1985) "Bloom's taxonomy and critical thinking instruction." *Educational Leadership 42*, 8, 36–39.

Paul, R., Binker, A., Jensen, K., and Kreklau, H. (1990) *Critical Thinking Handbook: A Guide for Remodeling Lesson Plans in Language Arts, Social Studies, and Science*. Rohnerl Park, CA: Foundation for Critical Thinking.

Pearson, P. (1982) *A Context for Instructional Research on Reading Comprehension*. Champaign, IL/Cambridge, MA: Bolt, Beranek and Newman.

Pinker, S. (1994) *The Language Instinct*. New York: HarperCollins.

Pogrow, S. (1988) "Teaching thinking to at-risk elementary students." *Educational Leadership 45*, 7, 79–85.

Powers, M. (ed.) (2000) *Children with Autism: A Parents' Guide*, 2nd edn. Bethesda, MD: Woodbine House.

Prawat, R. and Floden, R. (1994) "Philosophical perspectives on constructivist views of learning." *Educational Psychology 29*, 1, 37–48.

Premack, D. (1970) "A functional analysis of language." *Journal of the Experimental Analysis of Behavior 14*, 1, 1–19.

Presseisen, B. (1986) "Critical thinking and thinking skills: State of the art definitions and practice in public schools." Paper presented at the Annual Meeting of the American Educational Research Association in San Francisco, CA, April.

Prizant, B. (1982) "Speech-language pathologists and autistic children. What is our role? Part II, Working with parents." *ASHA Journal 24*, 531–537.

Prizant, B. and Rubin, G. (1999) "Contemporary issues in interventions for autism spectrum disorder: A commentary." *Journal of the Association of Severely Handicapped 24*, 3, 199–208.

Prizant, B. and Wetherby, A. (1987) "Communicative intent: A framework for understanding social-communicative behavior in autism." *Journal of the American Academy of Child Psychiatry 26*, 472–479.

Prizant, B. and Wetherby, A. (1989) "Enhancing language and communication in autism: From theory to practice." In G. Dawson (ed.) *Autism: Nature, Diagnosis, and Treatment*. New York: Guilford Press, pp.282–309.

Prizant, B. and Wetherby, A. (eds) (2000) *Autism Spectrum Disorders: A Transactional Developmental Perspective*. Baltimore, MD: Paul H. Brookes.

Prizant, B., Wetherby, A., Rubin, A., Laurent, P., and Quinn, J. (2003) *The SCERTS Model: Jenison Autism*. Grand Rapids, MI: Gray Center.

Quill, K. (1997) "Instructional considerations for young children with autism: The rationale for visually aided instruction." *Journal of Autism and Developmental Disorders 27*, 697–714.

Rakoff, D. (2002) "Brain Works." *New York Times*, 15 September.

Rapin, I. (2001) "An eight-year-old boy with autism." *Journal of American Medical Association 285*, 13, 1749–1757.

Rapin, I. and Dunn, M. (1997) "Language disorders in children with autism." *Seminars in Pediatric Neurology 4*, 86–92.

Redfearn, S. (2003) "Seeking the first signs of autism." *Washington Post*, 15 April, HE01.

Redfield, D. and Rousseau, E. (1981) "A meta-analysis of experimental research on teacher questioning behavior." *Review of Educational Research 51*, 237–245.

Reis, S., Burns, D., and Renzulli, J. (1992) *Curriculum Compacting: The Complete Guide to Modifying the Regular Curriculum for High Ability Students.* Mansfield Center, CT: Creative Learning Press.

Renzulli, J. (1988) "The multiple menu model for developing differentiated curriculum for the gifted and talented." *Gifted Child Quarterly 32*, 298–309.

Resnick, L. (1987) *Education and Learning to Think.* Washington, DC: National Academy Press.

Resnick, L. and Klopfer, L. (eds) (1989) *Towards the Thinking Curriculum: Current Cognitive Research.* Alexandria, VA: ASCD Yearbook.

Rhode Island State Advisory Committee on Gifted and Talented Education (2003) "Characteristics and behaviors of the gifted." www.ri.net/gifted_talented/character.html (accessed July 11, 2003).

Rice, M. (1980) *Cognition to Language: Categories, Word Meanings, and Training.* Baltimore, MD: University Park Press.

Rider, M. (1997) *The Rhythmic Language of Health and Disease.* St. Louis, MO: MMB Music.

Rimland, B. (1964) *Infantile Autism: The Syndrome and Its Implications for Neural Theory of Behavior.* New York: Appleton-Century-Crofts.

Rimland, B. and Fein, D. (1988) "Special talents of autistic savants." In L. Obler and D. Fein (eds) *The Exceptional Brain: Neuropsychology of Talent and Special Abilities.* New York: Guilford Press.

Rincover, A. and Koegel, R. (1977) "Classroom treatment of autistic children II: Individualized instruction in a group." *Journal of Abnormal Child Psychology 5*, 2, 113–126.

Risley, T. and Wolf, M. (1967) "Establishing functional speech in echolalic children." *Behavior Research Therapy 5*, 73.

Roedell, W. (1984) "Vulnerabilities of highly gifted children." *Roeper Review 6*, 127–130.

Rogers, K. and Silverman, L. (1997) "A study of 241 profoundly gifted children." Paper presented at the National Association for Gifted Children, 44th Annual Convention, Little Rock, AK, November.

Rogers, S. (1996) "Early intervention in autism." *Journal of Autism and Developmental Disorders 26*, 243–246.

Rogers, S. (1998) "Empirically supported comprehensive treatments for young children with autism." *Journal of Clinical Child Psychology 27*, 168–179.

Rogge, C., Galloway, J., and Welge, J. (1991) *Setting the Stage: A Practitioner's Guide to Integrating Vocational and Academic Education.* Springfield, IL: Illinois State Board of Education.

Romski, M. and Sevcik, R. (1996) *Breaking the Speech Barrier: Language Development Through Augmented Means.* Baltimore, MD: Paul H. Brookes.

Rosenthal, R. and Jacobsen, L. (1968) *Pygmalion in the Classroom.* New York: Holt, Rinehart and Winston.

Rothstein, E. (2002) "Myths about genius." *New York Times*, 5 January.

Rutter, M. (ed.) (1971) *Infantile Autism: Concepts, Characteristics and Treatment.* Baltimore, MD: Williams and Wilkins.

Rydell, P. and Prizant, B. (1995) "Assessment and intervention strategies for children who use echololia." In K. Quill (ed.) *Teaching Children with Autism: Strategies to Enhance Communication and Socialization.* New York: Delmar, pp.105–129.

Sacks, O. (1985) *The Man Who Mistook his Wife for a Hat and Other Clinical Tales*. New York: Touchstone.

Sacks, O. (1995) *An Anthropologist on Mars: Seven Paradoxical Tales*. London: Picador.

Sage, D. and Burrello, L. (1994) *Leadership in Educational Reform: An Administrator's Guide to Changes in Special Education*. Baltimore, MD: Paul H. Brookes.

Samples, R. (1976) *The Metaphoric Mind*. Reading, MA: Addison-Wesley.

Sawyer, R. (1990) *The Way of the Story Teller*. New York: Penguin.

Schopler, E., Lansing, M., and Waters, L. (1983) *Individual Assessment and Treatment for Autistic and Developmentally Disabled Children. Vol. 3: Teaching Activities for Autistic Children*. Austin, TX: Pro-Ed.

Schopler, E. and Mesibov, G. (eds) (1992) *High Functioning Individuals with Autism*. New York: Plenum Press.

Schopler, E. and Mesibov, G. (eds) (1995) *Learning and Cognition in Autism*. New York: Plenum Press.

Schopler, E., Mesibov, G., and Hearsey, K. (1995) "Structured teaching in the TEACCH system." In E. Schopler and G. Mesibov (eds) *Learning and Cognition in Autism*. New York: Plenum Press, pp.243–268.

Schopler, E., Mesibov, G., Shigley, R., and Bashford, A. (1984) "Helping autistic children through their parents: The TEACCH model." In E. Schopler and G. Mesibov (eds) *The Effects of Autism on the Family*. New York: Plenum Press, pp.65–81.

Schopler, E. and Reichler, R. (1971) "Parents as cotherapists in the treatment of psychotic children." *Journal of Autism and Childhood Schizophrenia 1*, 87–102.

Schopler, E., Short, A., and Mesibov, G. (1989) "Relation of behavioral treatment to 'normal functioning': Comment on Lovaas." *Journal of Consulting and Clinical Psychology 57*, 162–164.

Schuler, A., Prizant, B., and Wetherby, A. (1997) "Enhancing language and communication: Pre-language approaches." In D. Cohen and F. Volkmar (eds) *Handbook of Autism and Pervasive Developmental Disorders*, 2nd edn. New York: Wiley, pp.539–571.

Schuler, A. and Wolfberg, P. (2000) "Promoting peer play and socialization: The art of scaffolding." In A. Wetherby and B. Prizant (eds) *Autism Spectrum Disorders: A Developmental Transactional Perspective*. Baltimore, MD: Paul H. Brookes, pp.251–257.

Schultheis, S., Boswell, B., and Decker, J. (2000) "Successful physical activity programming for students with autism." *Focus on Autism and Other Developmental Disabilities 15*, 3, 159–162.

Schwartz, I., Boulware, G., McBride, B., and Sandall, S. (2001) "Functional assessment strategies for young children with autism." *Focus on Autism and Other Developmental Disabilities 16*, 4, 222–227.

Segal, M. and Adcock, D. (1981) *Just Pretending: Ways to Help Children Grow through Imaginative Play*. Upper Saddle River, NJ: Prentice-Hall.

Sekeles, C. (1996) *Music: Motion and Emotion: The Developmental Integrative Model in Music Therapy*. St. Louis, MO: MMB Music.

Shedlock, M. (1951) *The Art of the Story-Teller*. New York: Dover.

Shloino, S., Rapin, I., Arnold, S., Tuchman, R., Shulman, L., Ballaban-Gill, K., *et al.* (2001) "Language regression in childhood." *Pediatric Neurology 24*, 185–191.

Shoemaker, B. (1989) "Integrative education: A curriculum for the twenty-first century." *OSSC Bulletin 33*, 2.

Shoemaker, B. and Lewin, L. (1993) "Curriculum and assessment: Two sides of the same coin." *The Changing Curriculum 50*, 8, 55–57.

Silverman, L. and Kearney, K. (1989) "Parents of the extraordinarily gifted." *Advanced Development Journal 2*, 1, 41–56.

Simpson, R. (1999) "Early intervention with children with autism: The search for best practices." *Journal of the Association for Persons with Severe Handicaps 24*, 3, 218–221.

Simpson, R. and Myles, B. (1998) "Understanding and responding to the needs of students with autism." In R. Simpson and B. Myles (eds) *Educating Children and Youth with Autism.* Austin, TX: Pro-Ed.

Simpson, R. and Smith Myles, B. (eds) (1998) *Educating Children and Youth with Autism: Strategies for Effective Practice.* Austin, TX: Pro-Ed.

Sizer, T. (1984) *Horace's Compromise.* Boston, MA: Houghton Mifflin.

Sizer, T. (1991) *Horace's School: Redesigning the American High School.* Boston, MA: Houghton Mifflin.

Skrtic, T. (1991) "The special education paradox: Equity as the way to excellence." *Harvard Educational Review 61*, 2, 148–205.

Slavin, R. (1987) "Synthesis of research on cooperative learning." *Educational Leadership 38*, 8, 655–660.

Slavin, R. (1987) "Mastery learning reconsidered." *Review of Educational Research 57*, 175–214.

Slavin, R. (1989) "On mastery learning and mastery teaching." *Educational Leadership 46*, 7, 77–79.

Slobin, D. (1973) "Cognitive prerequisites for the development of grammar." In C. Ferguson and D. Slobin (eds) *Studies of Child Language Development.* New York: Holt, Rinehart and Winston, pp.175–208.

Slobin, D. (1974) *Psycholinguistics.* Glenview, IL: Scott, Foresman.

Smith, S. (1983) *The Great Mental Calculators.* New York: Columbia University Press.

Smith, T. (2001) "Discrete trial training in the treatment of autism." *Focus on Autism and Other Developmental Disabilities 16*, 2, 86–92.

Smutny, J. (2002) *Integrating the Arts into the Curriculum for Gifted Students.* ERIC No. 470524. Arlington, VA: ERIC Clearinghouse on Disabilities and Gifted Education.

Soloman, D., Watson, D., Battistch, V., Schaps, E., and Delucchi, K. (1992) "Creating a caring community: Educational practices that promote children's prosocial development." In F. Oser, A. Dick, and J. Party (eds) *Effective and Responsible Teaching: The New Synthesis.* San Francisco: Jossey-Bass.

Sousa, D. (2001) *How the Special Needs Brain Learns.* Thousand Oaks, CA: Corwin Press.

Spolin, V. (1986) *Theater Games for the Classroom.* Evanston, IL: Northwestern University Press.

Stainback, S., Stainback, W., and Forest, M. (eds) (1989) *Educating All Students in the Mainstream of Regular Education.* Baltimore, MD: Paul H. Brookes.

Sternberg, R. (1985) *Beyond IQ.* New York: Cambridge University Press.

Sternberg, R. and Davidson, J. (1986) *Conceptions of Giftedness.* New York: Cambridge University Press.

Strain, P. (1983) "Generalization of autistic children's social behavior change: Effects of developmentally integrated and segregated settings." *Analysis and Intervention in Developmental Disabilities 3*, 23–34.

Strain, P. and Schwartz, I. (2001) "ABA and the development of meaningful social relations for young children with autism." *Focus on Autism and Other Developmental Disabilities 16*, 21, 120–128.

Strike, K. (1975) "The logic of learning by discovery." *Review of Educational Research 45*, 3, 461–483.

Suddendorf, T. and Fletcher-Flinn, C. (1997) "Theory of mind and the origins of divergent thinking." *Journal of Creative Behavior 31*, 169–179.

Sumner, W. (1906) *Folkways: A Study of Mores, Manners, Customs, and Morals.* New York: Dover.

Tanguay, P. (2000) "Pervasive developmental disorders: A 10-year review." *Journal of the American Academy of Child and Adolescent Psychiatry 39*, 9, 1079–1095.

uis, MO: MMB Music.

an Antonio, TX: University of

gifted child in school." *Gifted*

General Psychiatry 23, 431.

University of Chicago Press.

Improvement (1993) *National*

US Government Printing Of-

Paper presented to the Austra-

Adelaide, South Australia.

man, L., and Foster, W. (1991)

fferentiating Curriculum for Gifted

tion No. S510. Arlington, VA:

ote inclusive schooling." In W.

chooling: *Interdependent Integrated*

drome." In A. Klin, F. Volkmar,

rd Press, pp.25–71.

D. (1987) "Social deficits in au-

Behavior Scales." *Journal of the*

niversity Press.

er.

Longman.

ene, OR: ERIC Clearinghouse

1 12).

rt *Rope Jingles for Active Learning.*

iscovery of an intellectual gift."

New York: Cambridge Univer-

ed Child. Moorabbim, Victoria:

Children from Birth to Adulthood.

munication development in au-

Autism: Identification, Education,

ociates, Inc.

rs: A Developmental Transactional

ative, social-affective, and sym-

velopmental disorder." *American*

Wetherby, A., Schuler, A., and Prizant, B. (19
    retical foundations." In D. Cohen and F.
    mental Disorders, 2nd edn. New York: W

Wiggins, G. (1990) The Case for Authentic Asse
    328 611. Arlington, VA: ERIC Clearin

Wilbarger, P. (1995) "The sensory diet: Act
    Sensory Integration Special Interest Section

Willard-Holt, C. and Holt, D. (1998) Applying
    IQ Score. Manassas, VA: Gifted Educatio

Willey, L.H. (1999) Pretending to be Normal: Li
    Publishers.

Wilson, E. (1998) Consilience: The Unity of K

Wing, L. (1976) Early Childhood Autism: Clinic

Wing, L. (1981) "Asperger's Syndrome: A cl

Winner, E. (1998) "Uncommon talents: Gifte
    Presents 9, 4, 32–37.

Wolf, M., Risley, T., and Mees, H. (1964) "A
    behavior problems of an autistic child."

Wolff, S. (1995) Loners: The Life Path of Unus

Yaffe, S. (1989) "Drama as a teaching tool."

Yanni (1994) "Reflections of passion." On Liv
    BWG Distributors.

Subject Index

Author Index

Armstrong, T. 16, 51

Bandura, A. 15
Bloom, B. 35, 46–7, 61–6
Bondy, A. 37, 75
Bruner, J. 66

Caine, G. 15, 16, 17
Caine, R. 15, 16, 17
Carroll, J. 79
Chard, S. 67
Collier, G. 43

Denes, P. 32
Dewey, J. 13, 15, 68, 98
Donnellan, A. 26

Fennimore, T. 68
Fox, R. 81
Freeman, B. 41
Frith, U. 15, 19–20, 38
Frost, L. 37, 75

Gardner, H. 15, 16, 51–3
Grandin, T. 21, 22, 38, 89–90, 92, 95, 97–8
Gray, C. 75
Green, G. 27, 81
Greenspan, S. 15, 81

Hamblin, R. 26
Harris, S. 26
Hart, C. 13, 33
Hermelin, B. 38
Hewett, F. 20, 26
Hodgson, L. 75
Hoerr, T. 53
Hunter, M. 74

Katz, L. 67
Kilpatrick, W. 66
Koegel, L. 26, 81
Koegel, R. 26, 81
Kovalik, S. 42
Kozloff, M. 20, 26

Krantz, P. 81
Krathwohl, D. 35, 47, 61

LaVigna, G. 26
Lazear, D. 16
Lissner, K. 32, 61–2
Lovaas, O. 20, 26, 80–1
Luce, S. 27

Mann, H. 13
Maurice, C. 27, 81
McClannahan, L. 81
McEachin, J. 81
McGee, G. 81
Montessori, M. 15, 66–7

National Research Council 21

O'Connor, N. 38
Olsen, K. 42

Park, C. 53
Park, J. 53
Pavlov, I. 26
Pinker, S. 12, 15
Pinson, E. 32
Premack, A. 25
Premack, D. 25, 43–4
Prizant, B. 81

Quill, K. 75

Skinner, B. 15, 26
Smith, T. 81
Sylwester, R. 15, 16, 63

Tinzmann, M. 68
Treffert, D. 14

Vysgotsky, L. 15

Watson 26
Weiss, M. 26
Wetherby, A. 81
Wieder, S. 15, 81
Wiggins, G. 64, 65
Wilmot, J. 19

125